Systemic Treatment of Families Who Abuse

Systemic Treatment of Families Who Abuse

Eliana Gil

Jossey-Bass Publishers · San Francisco

Substantial discounts on bulk quantities of Jossey-Bass books are available to corporations, professional associations, and other organizations. For details and discount information, contact the special sales department at Jossey-Bass Inc., Publishers. (415) 433–1740; FAX (800) 605–2665.

For sales outside the United States, please contact your local Simon & Schuster International Office.

TCF Manufactured in the United States of America on Lyons Falls Pathfinder Tradebook. This paper is acid-free and 100 percent totally chlorine-free.

Library of Congress Cataloging-in-Publication Data

Gil, Eliana, date.
    Systemic treatment of families who abuse / Eliana Gil.
        p.   cm. — (The Jossey-Bass social and behavioral science series)
    Includes bibliographical references and index.
    ISBN 0-7879-0153-9 (alk. paper)
    1. Child abuse—Treatment. 2. Family psychotherapy. 3. Abusive parents—Counseling of. I. Title. II. Series.
RC569.5.C55G558   1996
616.85'82230651—dc20

95-18734
CIP

HB Printing   10 9 8 7 6 5 4 3 2 1   FIRST EDITION

Contents

To
Dr. Robert Jay Green
and
Dr. Karen Saeger
for
tremendous professional guidance
and personal support

Introduction

I have worked in the area of child abuse prevention and treatment for the past twenty-one years. My initial work, beginning in 1973, focused on physical abuse and neglect. Child sexual abuse was discussed sporadically by professionals and lay people alike, but there was little indication then that this type of child abuse would take center stage for the next two decades.

Other things have changed over these years as well. The child abuse reporting laws have expanded to include new problem areas such as child prostitution and child pornography. Child kidnapping has become a tragic reality, and parents despair to find effective ways to protect their children, particularly since no place seems safe any longer. Child kidnappings have occurred in children's bedrooms, in child-care facilities, in out-of-home care settings, and in schools. More and more professionals have been added to the list of mandated reporters in an effort to immediately bring children considered to be at-risk to the attention of professionals who can take protective action.

The system that responds to allegations of child abuse has been overtaxed. Complaints abound about cases that are mishandled, maligning investigators for acting in a zealous, overprotective manner or for failing to take action, resulting in subsequent harm to children. Not only has there been an increase in the number of cases reported (more than 2.5 million in 1994), but the number of children and families referred for clinical services has also increased significantly, as has the number of studies on this topic.

The Single-Factor Theory

Research and clinical practice in the field of child abuse and neglect have been guided by theories about the causes of child maltreatment. The earliest theories emphasized single factors, particularly the characteristics of abusive or neglectful parents. Borrowing from the pathogenic (medical) model, early theories assumed that, since child maltreatment is an aberrant act, its perpetrators must also be aberrant in some way. The adoption of this approach resulted in the accumulation of a considerable amount of information about the personality characteristics and social and situational circumstances of people who mistreat children (Bonner, Kaufman, Harbeck, and Brassard, 1992). For example, research found that male incest offenders tend to be domineering and authoritarian and to have wives who are emotionally and sexually unavailable (see Cormier, Kennedy, and Sancowicz, 1973; Maisch, 1972; Raphling, Carpenter, and Davis, 1967), while physically abusive parents are often emotionally immature, chronically aggressive, and socially isolated (see Elmer, 1963; Merrill, 1962; Steele and Pollock, 1968).

As research efforts became more rigorous and focused, many studies suggested that widely accepted notions about the characteristics of offending parents had been derived from flawed research (see Finkelhor, 1984; National Research Council, 1993; Wolfe, 1991). A large proportion of the studies included small and often unrepresentative samples, used a retrospective methodology, and did not include comparison groups of nonabusing parents. Many of the studies on child sexual abuse, for example, relied on the memories of incarcerated offenders or others who had been brought to the attention of authorities.

Even when the research methodology was relatively sound and the results statistically significant, observed associations between parental characteristics and child maltreatment were not sufficiently strong to enable researchers or clinicians to use these characteristics to determine the likelihood that child maltreatment would occur (Gelles, 1982). In other words, the personality and situational characteristics identified by research were not consistent predictors of child abuse and neglect and did not accurately distinguish between parents who do and parents who do not mistreat their children. Indeed, many of the individual attributes associated with child maltreatment, such as low self-esteem, isolation from family and friends, and a childhood history of abuse, are also often found in parents who do not abuse or neglect their children (Belsky, 1980).

Finally, the few existing evaluations of interventions based on the pathogenic model (for example, Azar and Wolfe, 1989) found that clinical interventions were largely directed at the offending parent and were unsuccessful because they focused only on individual characteristics, which is not the best approach to understanding and eliminating child maltreatment because such maltreatment by definition involves interactions between parents and children (Wolfe, 1991). For these and other reasons, many authorities, including Gelles (1982), suggest: "While many clinicians and researchers search for simple answers to the complex problem of family violence, the research to date all too clearly points out that single-factor explanations of child abuse and family violence are inadequate, inaccurate and misleading" (p. 32).

The Ecological Theory

During the past two decades, new perspectives on the study of child maltreatment have emerged, concurrent with improvements in research methodologies. As a result, a number of multicausal explanations for the etiology of child maltreatment have been proposed. These explanations have been referred to collectively as "ecological," because they go beyond individual characteristics to consider factors in the broader environment in which child maltreatment occurs (Bronfenbrenner, 1977; National Research Council, 1993). Included in this category are the models developed by Belsky (1980), Cicchetti and Carlson (1989), Garbarino (1977), Trepper and Barrett (1989), Vander Mey and Neff (1986), and Wolfe (1991). Although ecological models focus on different types and aspects of child maltreatment, as pointed out by Holden, Willis, and Corcoran (1992), they share several important features: "Ecological models are concerned with identifying and specifying the effects of causal agents at multiple levels of the environmental context. Although individuals are considered to be important components, contextual influences at the levels of the family, community and culture are also emphasized. Ecological models assume multivariate causality and posit important interactional effects between components at different levels of the social ecological context" (p. 18). As this definition points out, ecological models regard child maltreatment not as the result of a single factor or system but as the consequence of interactions between multiple factors and systems.

Garbarino (1982), for instance, points out that "it is when personal vulnerability is compounded by social impoverishment that the most devastating effects take place" (p. 44). Two families might share similar parental risk factors for physical abuse, such as a childhood history of abuse, low frustration tolerance, depression, and unrealistic expectations about their children, but abuse occurs in only one of the families because the individual factors are accompanied by a lack of social support, marital discord, or chronic economic stress.

The importance of interacting factors is also reflected in Finkelhor's (1984, 1986) model of child sexual abuse. According to Finkelhor, four preconditions must be met for abuse to occur. The potential offender must (1) be motivated to sexually abuse a child, (2) overcome internal inhibitions against acting on that motivation, (3) overcome external barriers to commit a sexually abusive act, and (4) overcome the child's resistance to abuse. The presence or absence of each of these preconditions is determined by multiple individual, family, and environmental factors.

Many of the ecological models share in common a view of child maltreatment and its causes as dynamic rather than static phenomena. An important consequence of this view is a recognition of the impact of the child's developmental level on the potential for maltreatment. Factors that increase the probability for abusive and neglectful behavior among parents of infants may differ from the factors for parents of toddlers, school-age children, and adolescents. The likelihood of severe physical abuse, for instance, is greatest for toddlers and adolescents, apparently because of the special demands that characterize these two age groups, what Straus and Gelles (1986) call *oppositionality*. When parents do not have the capacities to deal effectively with children who are intent on asserting their autonomy, the probability for physical abuse can increase.

Recently, a growing number of experts have stressed the importance of considering child maltreatment as the result of developmental processes. As pointed out by the National Research Council (1993), "most forms of maltreatment are part of a pattern of maladaptive behavior that emerges over time" (p. 107). Investigators interested in the causes of child neglect, for instance, have confirmed the existence of a "vicious cycle of cumulative psychological risk" (Drotar, 1992, p. 121). Early neglect of an infant by a caretaker produces behaviors in the infant, such as feeding difficulties, irritability, and impaired social responsiveness, that place even greater demands on the caretaker, which then sets the stage for more severe neglect (Powell, Low, and Spears, 1987).

A developmental perspective also underlies Wolfe's (1987, 1991) "transitional model," which describes physical abuse as the endpoint of a series of stages that represent a gradual transformation in the parent-child relationship from milder to more harmful interactions. Wolfe argues that, without intervention, ineffective methods for controlling a child's behavior can gradually develop into the persistent use of harsh physical punishment.

Finally, the ecological models are distinguished from other explanations of child maltreatment by their recognition that abuse and neglect are the result of both the presence of risk factors and the absence of protective mechanisms (Cicchetti and Carlson, 1989). The existence of protective factors helps explain why attempts to identify high-risk parents through screening devices find a large proportion of the general population to be at risk for child maltreatment, while only a relatively small number of parents actually abuse or neglect their children (Garbarino, 1982). Apparently, many parents share personal and situational characteristics that can predispose them to child maltreatment, but a large number of parents are also protected by factors that counteract the effects of those characteristics.

The role of protective mechanisms is an important aspect of Wolfe's (1991) transitional model. According to Wolfe, mildly harmful interactions between a parent and child are much less likely to intensify when they are counteracted by such compensatory factors as positive social support, socioeconomic stability, and improvements in the child's behavior. Trepper and Barrett (1989) similarly propose that the likelihood of incest is reduced when a family has the coping (protective) mechanisms needed to deal effectively with the stresses that can precipitate this form of abuse. Among these coping mechanisms are an adequate social network, strong religious beliefs, and the availability of self-help groups such as Parents Anonymous.

Drawing on the work of both Tinbergen (1951) and Bronfenbrenner (1977), Belsky (1980) conceptualizes abuse as a social-psychological phenomenon that results from the interaction of factors located in four different levels, or systems, that are embedded within one another. The first level is *ontogenic development*, which refers to the characteristics that adults bring to the family setting and their roles as parents. A history of childhood abuse and/or excessive exposure to violence and a lack of information about child development are factors that place parents at higher risk for child maltreatment. The second level is the *microsystem*. It represents the family setting, or the "immediate context in which child maltreatment takes place" (Belsky, 1980, p. 321). At this level, factors that increase the probability for abuse or neglect include a high degree of marital conflict, role reversal between the parent and child, and a general state of household disorganization.

The *exosystem*, the third level, encompasses the informal and formal social structures that can affect the risk for child maltreatment. This level includes the school, the workplace, and the neighborhood. Specific factors associated with abuse and neglect include unemployment, chronic stress, and social isolation. Finally, the fourth level is the *macrosystem*. It represents the cultural values and beliefs that impinge, directly or indirectly, upon the ontogenic development of individual family members, the microsystem, and the exosystem. Of particular relevance at this level are society's attitudes toward violence, corporal punishment, and the status of children.

The Treatment of Child Abuse

Although there continues to be a paucity of treatment outcome models that conclusively establish the success of one therapeutic intervention over another, consensus exists about the fact that the treatment of child abuse is challenging and complex.

Several factors in particular appear clear. The treatment of child abuse differs from generic treatment in a variety of ways, not the least of which is the tremendous clinical responsibility in trying to alter harmful and potentially lethal behaviors while at the same time making efforts to preserve the family, without compromising children's safety. Clinicians working with child abuse must carefully assess the risk factors to maltreated children and take definitive protective action when and if necessary. Clinicians who have been trained to facilitate their clients' insight or motivation to make changes may feel pressured and uncomfortable at the prospect of more active clinical activity that asserts, insists on, and often imposes necessary changes.

In addition, trial and error has demonstrated the necessity for systemic rather than linear interventions. For example, in the early 1970s a standard response to physical abuse was to remove the child to an out-of-home care facility, such as a foster home or group home. Placement in and of itself was considered therapeutic, and abused children were not routinely referred for mental health services. The emphasis was on providing therapy for the abusive parent, with the domino principle in mind—that is, if parents could be helped to stop abusing their children, the children would inevitably benefit. Unfortunately, when children were reunited with their (supposedly rehabilitated) parents, all too often they were reabused and consequently placed in foster care anew.

The hypothesis that abusive parents could be helped to stop abusing and that their children would automatically benefit from foster placement and from their parents' rehabilitation was short-sighted at best. The thesis failed to recognize that children would not always react passively to foster placement, and that parents who were living without their children were by definition under less stress. The parenting skills they were learning were not put to the test, so it was difficult to predict if parents would be able to utilize these skills when their children were again underfoot. In addition, children in foster care were often angry or distrustful of their parents when they returned home, and reunifications were fraught with unanticipated conflict. It was simply insufficient to treat parents in isolation from their children, to fail to provide clinical services to children placed away from their parents, and to disregard the stress of reunification for both parents and children.

A more reasonable approach developed in the eighties, when researchers, educators, and clinicians began to give attention to parent-child interactions, as well as to the impact of both separation and reunification. Family therapists were consulted about the nature of reciprocity in relationships, and clinical services began to include, at the minimum, attention to the interactions among the abusive parent, the abused child, the nonabused siblings, and the nonabusive parent, who often contributed to the familial conflict.

In the nineties, the issue of child sexual abuse has become a dominant area of concern. In my experience, most child maltreatment books are written on this topic, most child abuse conferences address sex abuse issues, and so much research on child abuse focuses on this particular type that it might seem to an uninformed bystander that the issues of physical abuse, neglect, and psychological abuse must somehow be less critical.

Nothing could be further from the truth. Neglect continues to be the most reported form of child abuse, followed by physical abuse. In addition, no form of child abuse occurs without psychological damage. Children often live in violent, chaotic, or barren environments that produce grave emotional harm to them, as they watch one parent violate or injure the other, as they are exposed to inappropriate, explicit sexual behaviors, or as their parents withdraw physical attention and nurturing.

Physical abuse, sexual abuse, neglect, and psychological harm all have the potential to injure children, but as mentioned earlier, the particular consequences of child abuse depend on overlapping interactions between variables. Therefore, careful assessments must inform treatment plans that are comprehensive, directive, and cautious and that have measurable goals and objectives.

This book is for clinicians who want to be helpful to abusive or neglectful parents, and who want to feel more competent to address both the symptoms of child abuse and neglect and the underlying precipitating issues.

I will discuss both treatment successes and failures, and in the process I will share what I believe are critical aspects of treatment with families who abuse. I will promote a systemic approach, and advance interventions for all family members who I believe contribute to the maintenance of problem behavior in families, even though the family member who abuses retains 100 percent responsibility for starting and stopping the physical or sexual assault. In addition, I will discuss those variables that make treatment of child abuse unique, and I will offer directives for overcoming potential obstacles to successful treatment.

Since the treatment of child abuse and neglect must be concerned with dangerous behavior, the book will emphasize interventions focused on cognitive restructuring and behavioral change. However, cognitions and behaviors are greatly influenced by past experiences that may predispose individuals to seek out, avoid, or repeat familiar situations or relationships. I will therefore also touch on family-of-origin issues and unresolved traumata and the need to address these issues when they underlie, propel, or influence adult functioning, particularly in the area of parenting.

Acknowledgments

I would like to thank the many families with whom I have worked over the years, who showed extraordinary courage and perseverance. It is never easy to acknowledge problems, ask for and accept help, and then make difficult changes. I was allowed to contribute to the development of healthier and more rewarding family patterns, and for that I am grateful.

I would also like to thank my teachers at the California Graduate School of Family Psychology, for instilling in me a love for family therapy.

Alan Rinzler, my editor at Jossey-Bass, helped me organize my thoughts and clarify the ideas I propose in this book. It was our first collaboration, and I am deeply indebted to him for his gifted assistance. This was also my first collaboration with Monica Roizner-Hayes, who contributed to Chapter Five, and it was a great pleasure to work with her. In addition, I express my appreciation to

Dayan Edwards for her thorough research and summaries, part of which have been incorporated into this introduction.

I am blessed to have a loving husband who accepts the fact that I am often unavailable for periods of time while I write, and who is consistently supportive, bolstering my low morale when needed, and quietly caring for me when I'm fatigued, tired, or just plain cranky. We have created a physical and emotional environment that enlivens and sustains me. My daughter Teresa has also been patient and nurturing, always willing to play hooky when I needed a break, and keeping her music down low when I needed to work nearby. She is always willing to lend a friendly ear, and cheers me on with her unfailing pride.

Lastly, I thank Jeff Klein, my friend and tennis coach, because he helps me play better tennis and enjoy it more. Tennis, after all, provides the balance in my life that keeps me sane and optimistic.

Client confidentiality has been rigorously protected throughout this book. When presenting case examples, I have altered some combination of the client's age, gender, occupation, or other identifying information. When actual dialogue is provided, it is either reconstructed from memory using a variety of therapeutic conversations, or explicit permission was obtained to reproduce segments from actual therapy transcripts or from audio- or video-taped sessions.

Rockville, Maryland   ELIANA GIL
August 1995

Systemic Treatment of Families Who Abuse

1

What Makes Child Abuse Treatment Unique?

As stated in the introduction, clinicians need to view child abuse within an ecological perspective, intervening with individuals who live within social and cultural environments that are often stressful and challenging. The task of helping abusive parents seems overwhelming initially, since familial needs can be expansive. The most pressing clinical question is, How can we best be helpful to children and families?

Rather than promote specific theoretical paradigms (which research has failed to provide), in this chapter I will discuss the ways in which child abuse treatment is unique, and the type of interventions that I believe optimize our chances of being helpful.

Major Issues in Child Abuse and Neglect

In my experience, professionals who provide services to abusive families are guided by their own theoretical beliefs, which in turn point them to specific techniques, formats, and goal setting. For example, solution-focused therapists will select directive interventions designed to alter current behaviors in short amounts of time.

Psychodynamic approaches to child abuse may include long-term work and may emphasize the importance of parents' early experiences, seeking to make insight available for desired behavioral change. Eclectic clinicians, like myself, may tailor a treatment plan by drawing from an array of theoretical frameworks and weaving a clinical tapestry that addresses both past and current issues.

For example, although I initially concern myself with problematic parenting behaviors, I may quickly recognize that parental abuse stems from unresolved childhood trauma, and consequently encourage the parent to identify, acknowledge, and work through difficult past memories that might influence current parenting styles and approaches. If I decide to work on family-of-origin issues with an abusive parent, I remain cognizant of the fact that this work might exacerbate problematic parenting behaviors for a while, because a parent who is remembering and discussing his or her difficult childhood experiences may feel less empathetic to his or her own child, and may inadvertently repeat problem behaviors.

Child abuse and neglect issues may therefore be addressed with a variety of standard psychotherapeutic theories and techniques; however, these approaches must be braced by a number of specialized responses:

Child abuse therapy focuses on abusive behavior and provides immediate alternatives to maltreatment. Unlike generic treatment, in which clinical assessments unfold slowly and in which clinicians may use reflective or other nondirective techniques, working with people who abuse requires prompt, assertive interventions that direct clients to use safe and appropriate alternatives to their problematic or dangerous parenting behaviors.

Consider this example: I was supervising a graduate student via a one-way mirror during the student's initial interview of a mother who was referred to treatment by her pediatrician, who felt she was under "too much" stress.

THERAPIST: So, Mrs. S., tell me what brings you to therapy.

MOTHER: Well, my doctor thought it would be a good idea.

THERAPIST: Do you agree with your doctor?

MOTHER: Well, yes.

THERAPIST: Was it your physician?

MOTHER: Well, no, it was my kid's doctor.

THERAPIST: Tell me a little bit about why you think it's a good idea to see a therapist.

MOTHER: Well, it can't hurt.

THERAPIST: That's usually the case. How do you think it might help you?

MOTHER: Well, I feel almost embarrassed saying this, but I have a hard time, harder maybe than some, with my baby.

THERAPIST: How old is your baby?

MOTHER: Five weeks old, but it seems she's been there forever.

THERAPIST: And what's the hardest part about being a parent so far?

MOTHER: All of it, I think all of it is hard.

THERAPIST: Is there one thing that's hardest?

MOTHER: When she cries and won't stop for hours.

THERAPIST: Does that happen often?

MOTHER: All the time. That's why I took her to the doctor. I thought maybe there was something wrong with her. But the doctor just looks her over and tells me to be patient, that it will pass.

THERAPIST: In the meantime, it's probably hard to be patient.

MOTHER: I'll say.

THERAPIST: What do you do when she cries?

MOTHER: Mostly I try to take care of her. I feed her, but she spits up a lot. The doctor's given her two different kinds of milk.

THERAPIST: What else do you do?

MOTHER: I change her. Sometimes she's not even wet though, so I just change her diapers for the fun of it.

THERAPIST: Anything else?

MOTHER: Two or three times I've spanked her, but she just cries harder.

THERAPIST: So you've tried feeding her, changing her, spanking her, and still she cries. That must be frustrating for you.

MOTHER: Sometimes I'm sorry I had her.

THERAPIST: Really?

MOTHER: Yeah. [*Hesitates*] Do you think that's weird?

THERAPIST: No, not really.

MOTHER: You don't sound convinced.

THERAPIST: To be honest, I haven't worked with too many parents, and I don't have kids myself yet.

MOTHER: Oh great, so how are you supposed to help me?

THERAPIST: Well, I do know, I mean I've studied a lot about parenting, and as you know, I'll have a chance to discuss everything with my supervisor.

MOTHER: Well, I don't know. Maybe I should work with someone who knows more about being a parent.

At this point I decided to intervene, since the trainee had put herself in a defensive position and the interview had gotten off track. In particular, I was concerned that the mother had mentioned spanking her five-week-old infant, and that statement had remained intact.

I signaled the therapist-in-training to pick up the phone so we could talk. I told her that she needed to ask more about the mother's spanking of the child, and then she needed to state firmly that spanking was not an option. The therapist-in-training was feeling stressed during the interview and had heard but not heard what the mother had said about spanking.

I sensed her discomfort and guided her to ask about the two or three spankings, whether the parent had noticed bruises on the infant following the spanking, and then to make the statement about spanking being inappropriate and potentially dangerous for such a young child. I told her that many parents worry that no one will be able to help them, and the best way she could address that issue was to discuss parenting issues with the mother in a matter-of-fact way and regain some confidence about her ability to be helpful. The trainee then proceeded with the interview.

THERAPIST: I need to talk to you a little more about the spankings.

MOTHER: I've only done it three times.

THERAPIST: Tell me about those times.

MOTHER: What do you want to know?

THERAPIST: Well first of all, what was going on?

MOTHER: She was crying and crying and crying. I had let her cry for almost two hours, longer than I thought she could cry, and still she wouldn't stop.

THERAPIST: How did you feel when the crying was going on?

MOTHER: Frustrated, almost despaired.

THERAPIST: Did you feel angry?

MOTHER: Well, yes . . . but more than that, it was a feeling of exasperation, like this baby was trying to get to me.

THERAPIST: You mean because she was crying?

MOTHER: Yeah. I feel like she has me prisoner.

THERAPIST: Those are pretty strong feelings.

MOTHER: I told you I felt bad about it. My friends keep telling me it's normal to feel frustrated and it will pass as I get more comfortable being a mother, but I don't know.

THERAPIST: You don't know if you'll ever feel successful?

MOTHER: That's right.

THERAPIST: Well, one thing is for sure. You are certainly giving it a good try.

MOTHER: Well, yeah, I do keep trying, but sometimes I get so tired of it all.

THERAPIST: Do you have any help with the baby?

MOTHER: Not really. Sometimes my mom offers to come over and help, but when she's there I feel like she's watching and criticizing me.

THERAPIST: Does she know what to do when the baby cries?

MOTHER: I don't really know.

THERAPIST: Well, babies who cry a lot can certainly cause parents to feel tired and frustrated. I know that happens to a lot of parents.

MOTHER: Nobody I know.

THERAPIST: So most of your friends have had an easier time with their babies?

MOTHER: It seems that way to me.

THERAPIST: One thing I want to make sure I say before I forget is that it's really important that you don't spank your baby.

MOTHER: Excuse me.

THERAPIST: Earlier you talked about spanking your baby, and it's really important that you know that it's potentially dangerous to spank such a small baby.

MOTHER: Well, I don't hit her hard or anything.

THERAPIST: Any spanking with a baby so young can be dangerous, so I need to make sure you won't do that again.

MOTHER: Well . . . I guess I don't have to do that.

THERAPIST: What do you think you can do instead?

MOTHER: That's why I'm here. I don't know what else to do.

THERAPIST: Well, let's spend the rest of the time together talking about what you can do when you feel frustrated and tired, and how to do something other than spanking the child.

During the rest of the interview the trainee encouraged the mother to role play what she might try to do when the child was crying incessantly. Some of the ideas that emerged in the discussion included walking around the house with the baby, taking the baby for a walk outdoors, giving her a warm bath, playing music, placing the child in a safe place and going to another room, calling to talk to a friend, doing jumping jacks, or listening to a relaxation tape for a brief period.

This example illustrates how important it is both to set immediate limits on inappropriate behaviors and to encourage parents to generate realistic options that will replace inappropriate or dangerous responses. If parents are unable to generate options, I usually ask them if they have ever seen another parent function in a way they respected or thought more appropriate, and I may offer a number of suggestions that other parents have used and found helpful.

Therapy is goal oriented and solution focused. When treating abusive or neglectful families, clinicians must establish and maintain a focus on abuse or neglect. It is possible to allow generic therapy clients to become comfortable enough to bring up issues for discussion as they see fit, but clinicians who work with abusive and neglectful parents must by necessity be more active, setting agendas and insisting on clients' participation and cooperation.

When generic clients miss appointments, decide to attend sessions less frequently, or fail to complete homework assignments, clinicians may remain flexible and address these issues in a concerned but relaxed manner. Clinicians who work with abuse and neglect do not have these privileges, since the topic of abuse and neglect must be addressed immediately and consistently. Because children's lives are hanging in the balance, clinicians cannot be patient and flexible.

In the example of the mother who spanked her infant child, the clinician kept parenting issues in the forefront, tailoring the clinical interview so that the subject was reviewed during each session.

THERAPIST: How was your week?

MOTHER: Pretty good. The baby is beginning to quiet down a bit.

THERAPIST: Were there any times that she cried a lot and you felt helpless to quiet her?

MOTHER: It happened one time really bad and then a few other times it wasn't so bad.

THERAPIST: Let's talk about the really bad time, and then the other times as well.

MOTHER: What do you want to know?

THERAPIST: I want to know what happened when the baby cried. For example, what do you say to yourself as the baby starts crying?

MOTHER: Oh, I usually say "Oh, God, here we go again," or "There she goes again, the little brat."

THERAPIST: "Here we go again" means what exactly?

MOTHER: She cries, I get upset.

THERAPIST: So on the really bad time what happened?

MOTHER: I got so upset I nearly hit her again.

THERAPIST: How did you stop yourself?

MOTHER: I just remembered that I couldn't do that.

THERAPIST: Why not?

MOTHER: You said it might be dangerous.

THERAPIST: What do you think?

MOTHER: Well, until you said anything I hadn't really thought of it as dangerous, but later I thought that was right, because she's so little.

THERAPIST: So you've just removed that as a possible option.

MOTHER: Strange as that might sound.

THERAPIST: And what did you do instead?

MOTHER: Actually, I went into my bedroom and I lay on the bed and cried.

THERAPIST: How did you feel about doing that?

MOTHER: It felt good that I didn't have to stay with her while she cried, and it felt good to just let it out instead of trying to keep it bottled up inside.

THERAPIST: So crying in your room allowed you to feel some release.

MOTHER: Yeah.

THERAPIST: And what happened next?

MOTHER: Amazingly, she fell asleep and I went back into her room and covered her up, and I just looked at her.

THERAPIST: What did you think as you looked at her?

MOTHER: How pretty she is when she's sleeping.

THERAPIST: I can imagine. And it sounds like you were feeling more peaceful yourself.

MOTHER: Another time I tried having her listen to music, classical music, and although she didn't shut up for almost half the record, eventually she did, and there was something about humming along with the music that I really enjoyed.

THERAPIST: Good, good. So at least two techniques became effective for you, going to your room and crying, and playing music when the baby was crying.

MOTHER: Yeah. I feel like there's some hope.

THERAPIST: And most importantly, you didn't hit her again.

MOTHER: Yeah, I don't think I'll do that again.

THERAPIST: That's good, because there are lots of other ways of coping with frustration. We'll keep talking about this every time you come.

Therapy must focus on safety issues. Abusive and neglectful parents are referred to therapy to learn appropriate and safe parenting behaviors. Children may be allowed to remain in the home as long as parents participate in a treatment program, or they may be returned home only after their parents have made necessary changes in their caretaking skills.

Children's safety is a primary consideration for clinicians treating abusive or neglectful parents and rigorous efforts must be undertaken on children's behalf. Nonabusive clients may choose whether or not to bring their children to therapy, or they may disclose varying amounts of information about their children's general well-being, but clinicians who work with abusive or neglectful families must have access to the children. They may require their participation in treatment, and they must have the means to observe parent-child interactions or obtain third-party reports about the children. Other clients may assert their confidentiality privilege, refusing access to third parties; abusive or neglectful parents who are mandated to treatment are under strict adherence to imposed conditions, which is both an advantage and a disadvantage to the clinician. On the one hand, forcing parents to cooperate may create an environment of distrust and resistance; on the other hand, the clinical task of monitoring children's safety is made easier when parents are required to comply with treatment demands.

When working with abusive or neglectful families, clinicians must create opportunities for accountability through monitoring. This means that clinicians must explore the family's environment to locate individuals who have ongoing contact with family members and who might be in a position to provide collateral information. When appropriate, clinicians may also ask to meet with extended family members or spouses, with caretakers, or with school personnel, in an effort to ensure that children will be monitored and not become isolated. In the earlier example, the clinician obtained permission from the mother to talk with the pediatrician, who agreed to monitor the child's physical safety and reinforce clinical limits regarding spanking. The clinician told the mother that she would advise the pediatrician about the spanking and that he might also have additional advice about how to address the baby's crying in a positive way. The clinician also asked the mother to bring her child to a few therapy sessions in the hope that the child might cry and the feelings and behaviors elicited by the child's crying could be dealt with as they occurred.

One of the earliest lessons I learned about the importance of direct observation occurred when I was working with a couple who bitterly complained about their child's out-of-control behavior. The child came to therapy once with his parents and was so disruptive and destructive that my supervisor encouraged me to see the parents alone and offer them new parenting strategies to use with their child. I was a student of Parent Effectiveness Training (PET) at the time, and I felt that these parents were good candidates to use these techniques since they had demonstrated good impulse control and a willingness to experiment. In therapy sessions, we rehearsed the use of PET techniques in a number of problematic situations they had encountered with their child, but they reported that the child was getting worse instead of better. Finally, against my supervisor's better judgement, I asked the couple to bring their child to therapy, and we set up a task that would require them to experiment with their new techniques.

I was appalled to observe that although the parents used the words we had rehearsed calmly, when the child was present they shouted those words at the top of their lungs, with alarming hostility and a threatening physical posture that visibly frightened and overwhelmed the child. Their reports of how they were utilizing the techniques had been grossly inaccurate, because they had not described their pitch, tone, posture, and demeanor as they corrected their child. The boy's response to this threatening and controlling behavior was to become frightened and then to compensate by becoming more oppositional and defiant.

Therapy for child abuse perpetrators is usually mandatory. Parents who abuse or neglect do not seek help voluntarily but are actually often court ordered. Mandatory therapy is potentially difficult and adversarial. Feeling forced to do something may lead to hostility or feelings of helplessness. But although mandatory therapy is not the ideal situation, it is also not a futile one. Over the years, I have come to appreciate what can be accomplished within this context. At the very least, the situation has clarity; potentially, it can encourage families to make long-overdue changes designed to improve the quality of their interactions. It may take a little more time and effort under these circumstances to establish a therapeutic relationship; but gradually, therapy can proceed as if it were voluntary, because as parents recognize the usefulness of treatment, they may inadvertently grow to appreciate the outcome.

Clinicians who have been trained to discern, focus on, and encourage clients' motivation to change may feel disillusioned with abusive parents, who often deny any internal motivation to make changes, referring instead to external pressures that they often resist. It is possible for the therapist to feel defeated, hopeless, and frustrated unless clinical expectations regarding motivation are altered when working with families who abuse.

Therapy occurs within a multidisciplinary context. Traditionally, psychotherapists are trained to protect their clients' privacy at all costs, using extreme caution when contacting or when contacted by other professionals to discuss their clients. Mental health practitioners, particularly those in private settings, may have limited contact with other professionals (such as child protective services, probation, or the police) and may remain confused about the roles and responsibilities of other disciplines. Clinicians working with abusive or neglectful families will always work within a multidisciplinary context and this context must become familiar and comfortable to the clinician if he or she is to provide the most effective treatment services possible.

Clinicians may need to identify and convene other professionals working with an abusive or neglectful family in order to discuss the status of the family and conditions imposed by legal jurisdictions. If clinicians hope to provide useful treatment, they must obtain clarity about the family's predicament. Once clinicians hear directly from other professionals about the nature of the problem and what changes are expected and required, they can formulate appropriate treatment plans.

In my experience, one of the most consistent consultation questions has to do with how to coordinate the various services often provided to families who abuse. Taking an active lead in calling professional meetings, developing written contracts, and following up on commitments made by various professionals may increase the amount of time clinicians spend working with families who abuse. Doing this extra work may seem unfamiliar to many clinicians, who may feel that this adjunct work is inconsistent with their professional roles, but it is this willingness and ability to reach out and create an external system of support and monitoring that can lead to clinical success. Coordinating services may represent an initial investment of time, but it results in tremendous payoffs in terms of treatment success.

Child abuse therapy often involves life and death concerns and elicits powerful countertransference. Treating families who abuse places clinicians in the stressful position of making assessments and recommendations that are designed to keep families together or apart. Clinicians are often asked to offer opinions about a variety of issues, such as whether children can be returned home, or whether they must remain in foster care; whether parents have decreased their dangerous behaviors, or whether they remain volatile; whether parents can now provide a basic level of care for their children; and so on. Inevitably, clinicians struggle with these difficult situations and must offer their best educated guesses about family functioning. Clinicians cannot look into the future and predict how individuals will behave; they must gather sufficient hard data to render their most conservative professional judgment. Unfortunately, no matter how experienced the clinician, these decisions often take an emotional toll. In candid discussions with colleagues, we have often confided to each other our persistent concerns about former clients, long after formal therapy has terminated.

Countertransference responses occur fluidly and relentlessly. Clinicians must learn to manage a broad range of feelings, thoughts, perceptions, and attitudes that emerge in the context of working with families who abuse. They may alternately feel controlling and helpless, optimistic and hopeless, competent and incompetent, confident and frightened, angry and calm, elated and sad. These feelings may cause clinical overfunctioning, boundary violations, or premature terminations or referrals to other professionals. It is not unusual for therapists to feel as if they themselves have been victimized, or been victimizing, or as if they have rescued or helped to destroy a family. As a result, clinicians may choose to screen out families who abuse, choosing to work with more compliant or responsive clients rather than process difficult countertransference responses, thus fortifying themselves to provide useful and rewarding clinical services.

Therapy with families who abuse requires clinicians to have a working knowledge of community resources. Mental health professionals work in settings that are more or less involved with community programs and agencies. During my many years as a consultant, I have been baffled by the isolation and naïveté of many health care professionals who have seemed unaware of critical services such as shelters for battered women, emergency home services (homebuilders), respite care programs, hotlines, legal aid, free clinics, and so forth. Still other clinicians are cognizant that community programs exist and yet do not have a clue as to how to locate a single-parents group or Adult Children of Alcoholics group.

Clinicians working with abuse and neglect must identify and be willing to use the vast helping community that functions as a holding environment to provide crisis services and meet the many needs of families that no single professional can provide without developing feelings of futility or burnout. Specialized community services often fortify clinical efforts. A larger helping system can sustain a family's many needs so that no individual helper feels burdened or inundated. Families who abuse are multiproblem families who require a variety of complimentary services. Clinicians are often in a position to orchestrate the creation of this extended system which in the long run increases the family's receptivity to individual clinical efforts.

Therapy with families who abuse requires special handling of confidentiality issues, information-sharing, and adherence to reporting statutes. At the beginning of treatment I tell all clients about the limits of confidentiality, explaining that everything that goes on in therapy is private or privileged communication, with several noteworthy exceptions. I have prepared a consumer information form that discusses policies regarding this issue, as well as payment, cancellation, tardiness, and inappropriate sexual contact between client and therapist. The following excerpt from this "informed consent" form concerns the limits of confidentiality:

Psychotherapist-client communications are privileged and must be kept confidential. However, psychotherapists must adhere to legal duties which supersede confidentiality. Confidentiality may be waived under the following circumstances:

1. Child abuse and neglect. When clinicians have knowledge or reasonable suspicion that anyone is abusing or neglecting children, they are required by law to report such knowledge or suspicion. Child abuse is a generic term that includes various types of maltreatment such as physical or sexual abuse, neglect or child endangerment, willful cruelty or unjustifiable punishment of a child (including unjustifiable mental suffering), and child sexual exploitation (such as pornography or prostitution). The child abuse laws mandate professionals to report abuse of children by any person, including older children, parents, or other adults.

2. Elder abuse and abuse of developmentally disabled populations. This law was designed to protect any person eighteen

years and older whose physical or mental limitations prevent the person from protecting himself or herself from physical or sexual abuse, financial exploitation, assault, or other forms of harm.

3. The threat of harm. The law imposes a legal duty to notify police and intended victims whenever a patient is threatening to commit lethal harm to a known specific person. The original "Tarasoff" case arose from a situation in which a man confided to his psychologist that he was going to kill a former girlfriend and then proceeded to do so. The court ruled that mental health professionals must notify police and intended victims of specific lethal threats in order to maximize the chances that the intended victim can be protected.

4. The danger of suicide. The clinical duty to take protective action when a client is suicidal is not legal but ethical. Clinicians must make active efforts through aggressive suicide assessments, crisis intervention strategies, suicide contracts, increased clinical sessions, notification of immediate family, encouraging the person to admit himself or herself for psychiatric observation, or contacting police to take the person to an emergency room for psychiatric assessment for involuntary confinement (5150) if the person is considered to be a risk to self or others.

After I review these limits and the other general information included on the form, I obtain the client's signature on an original and on a copy of the form. The client takes the signed copy home and I keep the original in his or her file.

Reviewing such a form is a great opportunity to clarify what is and what is not child abuse, to clarify what will and will not be reported, and to articulate a focused, above-board, and clear approach to working with the problems of child abuse and neglect. Such an open discussion does not seem to hinder parental disclosure regarding difficulties in the home. Paradoxically, many parents alert clinicians (either through verbal clues or behavior) to abuse or neglect problems because on some level they want help to stop the abusive behavior. The parents' behavior can therefore be understood as "action language" that communicates their most private or censored thoughts and feelings. Parents who are told that their child will be removed if the child has one more bruise are asking for the child's removal if they bring the child into therapy covered with unexplained bruises. Although parents may not be able to admit to themselves or others that they want their child to be removed, they may cause the desired effect through their behavior.

When clinicians must make required child abuse reports, there are a few approaches that can minimize negative parental reactions. First, the reporting law can be used as an external limit that is often necessary to control unacceptable parental behavior. Parents who abuse physically or sexually cannot control or adjust their caretaking behaviors and do not seem capable of regulating internal controls to constrict their harmful behaviors. Parents who neglect seem unable or unwilling to provide necessary caretaking behaviors to their children. The child abuse reporting law clearly sets limits and may yield sufficient power to "shake up" the status quo regarding unacceptable or harmful childrearing practices. At a minimum, outside intervention often causes parents to reflect on their situation, and may induce sufficient concern or fear to motivate positive changes.

Reporting child abuse can also be a helpful strategy to help parents alter their harmful behavior. When clinicians recognize the law's important intent, they can introduce the process of reporting child abuse in a matter-of-fact, nonadversarial way: "I am going to make a referral to child protective services because I am concerned that you are hurting your child and that in doing so you are hurting yourself. I know you don't feel good about what you're doing and you've told me about it [or shown me] because you want me to help you stop. You want to be safe from hurting your child and most of all I'm sure that you want your child to be safe. To do this, I will first call child protective services."

I believe it is both worthwhile and effective to give parents a chance to talk to child protective services themselves. Once I have informed them that I will call child protective services, I invite them to talk to the child protective services worker on the phone. Usually this invitation confuses parents, but in the long run it might actually help the treatment process, as illustrated in the following example in which a mother tells the therapist that both she and her children are being physically abused by her violent husband:

THERAPIST: . . . So for all those reasons I will be talking to child protective services about what's going on in your family.

MOTHER: What is going to happen to my kids? Will they take them away from us?

THERAPIST: I can't answer that question. Removing children is one of the options that the courts have, but they tend to remove children if they believe that they are in imminent danger, which usually means there's no one to protect them. I believe that you are very concerned about your children and definitely want the abuse to stop.

MOTHER: I've been sick by what's happened.

THERAPIST: I sense that, and I think that's why you came to therapy. Deep down you wanted someone to help you keep your kids safe from your husband's beatings.

MOTHER: As long as he keeps drinking, he's like somebody I don't even know. Oh, my God, I don't know how he will react.

THERAPIST: I know. From what you've told me, you have reason to be concerned, and it will be important to let protective services know about that, that he gets out of control when he's drinking.

MOTHER: Every now and then he breaks down and apologizes to the kids and I. . . .

THERAPIST: It sounds like a part of him is aware of the pain that he's causing his family.

MOTHER: He's basically a good person.

THERAPIST: I think you're both basically good people, and you in particular are focused on being a good and responsible parent who protects her children from harm.

MOTHER: This is one of the hardest things I've ever gone through.

THERAPIST: I understand. I think you've taken an important first step toward helping yourself and your kids, and now I'd like to suggest that you take another important step.

MOTHER: What's that?

THERAPIST: Well, I would like to give you the chance of talking to child protective services yourself. I know that I could call them and tell them what I think is going on, but you know much better than I do how to explain the situation.

MOTHER: I don't know if I could do that.

THERAPIST: It's your choice, of course. I just usually like to give parents the chance to talk to child protective services so that they don't feel that someone's talking behind their back, or so that they can get their questions answered right away.

MOTHER: I'm so embarrassed. Gosh . . . I don't know.

THERAPIST: What are you most embarrassed about?

MOTHER: About the whole thing, everything. I can't believe I've let it go so far. I should have done something last year when he first beat me in front of the kids.

THERAPIST: Well, from what we've discussed it seems that you've made lots of efforts to try to stop the abuse on your own. You've talked to him, you've talked to his parents, you've given him books to read, you've gotten the phone numbers and addresses of local AA groups.

MOTHER: Yeah, but. . . .

THERAPIST: Do you think there are other things you could have done?

MOTHER: I wish I could have spared the kids. . . .

THERAPIST: I know. It's been hard for them to feel frightened for themselves and for you. And you need to focus on what steps you're taking now, because the past is the past and you can't go back and change it. I think you wanted to keep your family together and hoped that he would change. It's often what parents do. I think you now realize that you need to do something more, something different.

MOTHER: Unfortunately. . . .

THERAPIST: So, we can do it either way. I can dial the phone, get a worker on the line, and then you can talk to the person, or I can talk to them directly while you listen.

MOTHER: What do you think I should do?

THERAPIST: Whatever you feel comfortable doing.

MOTHER: Can I tell you what to ask them?

THERAPIST: Sure, I'll try to get as much information as you want, or you can ask them yourself directly.

MOTHER: Okay, I'll talk to them, but if I get somebody rude or mean on the phone, you can talk to them.

THERAPIST: Sounds fair. I'll handle the rude, mean person.

MOTHER: What will I tell them?

THERAPIST: Just tell them about what happened this weekend and how your kids have bruises on their backs and stomachs.

MOTHER: Should I tell them about my black eye?

THERAPIST: Yes.

MOTHER: What will they think?

THERAPIST: That you're a parent in a difficult situation, trying to protect your kids. I'll get them on the line.

At this point I called child protective services and luckily got a very sensitive and soft-spoken worker on the line who put the parent at ease almost immediately. The parent told the worker about her husband's drinking, how he had beaten her off and on for a year, and how the past weekend he had turned on the children and given them a beating that she was able to stop but only after the children incurred injuries. She asked the worker what would happen and if there was some way to keep her kids safe since she expected he would not take kindly to her calling the authorities. She also asked about time frames and about how quickly or slowly things would happen.

I heard the mother say she would not need a shelter since she had a cousin nearby she could stay with. I also heard the mother tell the workers that the children were at school, and no, she had not taken them to the pediatrician, not because she didn't think they were badly hurt, but mostly because she didn't know how to explain their bruises.

After providing the children's names, ages, and school address, the conversation was coming to an end so I asked to speak to the worker. I introduced myself and reiterated the mother's concern about the children's safety. I also mentioned that the mother had been in therapy for almost six months and that she was planning to continue to attend therapy. The mother had also asked for a referral for the children. I told the worker that I would fill out a standard Department of Justice form and that I would send it to her shortly (within the required thirty-six hours).

The mother appeared reassured and empowered by talking to child protective services herself. Even though it may make parents briefly uncomfortable, giving them the opportunity to speak on their own behalf may actually allow them to feel more actively involved in the protection of their children. This may also help parents feel less victimized, helpless, or frightened.

If parents do not wish direct contact with child protective services at a particular time, I make the telephone report in front of them so that they hear exactly what I say. In this way, I can emphasize my areas of concern and present an organized explanation of the factors that have caused me to have reasonable suspicion. Since I have already been clear about these factors with the parents, it allows me to demonstrate consistency and to be seen as a trustworthy helper.

On occasion, parents have refused both options and chosen to leave the therapy altogether, often feeling betrayed, frightened, or angry. If parents become threatening to either the clinician, the spouse, or the children, I will immediately communicate this threat to child protective services so they can take appropriate action. A few times, not only did the nonabusive parent obtain a restraining order against the spouse, but it was also necessary for me to obtain a restraining order from an irate, out-of-control parent.

Not all abusive parents respond cooperatively when child abuse reports are made. Some parents file lawsuits for slander. One parent filed a nuisance complaint against a colleague of mine because she had failed to submit the written report within the specified thirty-six hours. Professionals have immunities for making child abuse reports as required by law, but this immunity does not prevent the filing of lawsuits. Although no professional has ever been successfully litigated for making a child abuse report, some professionals have been held liable for failing to make required child abuse reports.

In spite of the fact that therapists have not been successfully sued for making child abuse reports as required, these lawsuits can be emotionally and financially draining since they often require that clinicians hire attorneys, respond to subpoenas for records, or give lengthy depositions. In addition, insurance carriers are routinely notified when lawsuits are filed and in some cases just the fact that clinicians answer "yes" to a question about whether anyone has ever filed a lawsuit against them, the insurance company raises their premium.

Mental health professionals have a legal duty to report suspected child abuse, but most nonprofessional citizens (including parents) are not required to make child abuse reports and may do so at their discretion, although they may feel ethical obligations to file such reports. The mental health professional does not adhere to his or her legal duty to report if he or she instructs parents to make child abuse reports on their own and does not fill out a reporting form as dictated by law. I have consulted with clinicians who have chosen to delegate their reporting responsibilities to parents who have agreed to file a report but who have in fact never called protective agencies. The mental health professional must ensure that he or she has complied with the law by filing the report by phone and in writing within the specified period.

Providing treatment services to families who abuse and neglect is complex and multifaceted. One of the most relevant factors, mentioned earlier, is that clients do not seek services voluntarily. Clinicians are challenged to find ways to assist individuals who do not want assistance and who often find their behavior ego-syntonic. In addition, it is characteristic of parents who abuse to deny their behaviors, either because they feel guilty or remorseful, fear legal repercussions, or feel entitled to behave as they wish with their children.

Clinicians must therefore create a context for change and address issues of denial in such a way that clients eventually decrease their denial in favor of participation. This usually occurs once the family experiences clinical empathy, understanding, and concrete assistance, rather than abstract attempts at being helpful. This book will discuss ideas for addressing resistance and denial, providing concrete help to families who abuse, working within a multidisciplinary context with full use of adjunctive community services, and focusing on children's safety.

2

Assessment

When families with parenting problems are referred for therapy, clinicians first need to determine the presence and extent of risk factors, which will in turn allow for clinical recommendations about the possibility of children remaining in the home during the course of treatment, if indeed the family is seen as amenable to treatment.

Friedrich (1990) states that treatment effectiveness for children is greatly enhanced when the following conditions exist:

Ongoing support of the child is provided by a primary parent figure.

A sense of safety has been or is being established for the child to protect against future victimization.

The therapy with the child is occurring concurrently with therapy that is creating systems change (for example, therapy for both parents), and the nonabusing parent is having regular contact with the child's therapist.

The therapist is skillful, goal oriented, conceptually clear, and willing to be directive in a supportive manner.

The child is able to communicate regarding the abuse and can tolerate the intensity of the therapy process.

Friedrich's conditions enhance the effectiveness of family treatment as well, since systemic efforts endeavor to ascertain children's safety, engage the family's participation in treatment, and concentrate on creating change in interactional family patterns sufficient to correct or enhance parenting.

Risk Factors

Although it is impossible to accurately predict whether individuals who behave in dangerous, volatile, or violent ways are likely to continue these aggressive behaviors in the future, it is possible to render a professional opinion about the likelihood of reoccurrence based on the presence and extent of risk factors.

Risk factors can be considered within three categories discussed by Stickrod Gray and Pithers (1993): predisposing, precipitating, and perpetuating factors. *Predisposing factors* stem from past experience and may contribute to an individual's current difficulties. For example, a parent's alcoholism may predispose a child to a drinking problem, due both to genetic factors and to modeling. Although there is no evidence of a linear cause and effect between a parent's alcoholism and a child's later alcoholism (in fact, some children who grow up with alcoholic parents develop strong convictions against drinking), parental alcoholism might be considered a predisposing factor to substance abuse problems in some individuals. Likewise, a young adult who has been beaten all his life may be predisposed toward violent vocal outbursts and physical displays of violence. Conversely, as in the previous example, some youngsters who have been abused may become extremely timid and hesitant to acknowledge or exhibit any outward displays of anger.

Precipitating factors occur prior to and may actually elicit the problem behavior. Many parents who abuse relate precipitating events that they perceived as conflictual and which contributed to their acting-out behavior. For example, a mother who was demoted at work and is nursing a flu has an altercation with a child care worker, comes home to find that her oldest daughter has not made dinner, has not cleaned the house as instructed, and has broken one of the mother's favorite glasses. Suddenly, the mother feels frustrated and angry. What happened at work, plus her physical illness, may predispose her to irritability, and her perception that her daughter is making things harder for her may precipitate a violent outburst.

Perpetuating factors are those that contribute to continuity of a problem. Predisposing and precipitating factors can cause the emergence of a problem, but what causes a problem is different from what sustains it.

Let's look again at the example of the sick, overwhelmed mother. After she slaps her teenage daughter and yanks her younger daughter by the arm and sticks her in her room, she retires to her own bedroom and cries. Shortly thereafter she gets up, cleans the house, makes dinner, and asks both her daughters to come eat. During dinner, normalcy is restored. No one discusses what happened earlier and it is as if it never occurred—until the next time. The mother's inability to set limits with her older daughter, or to impose consequences for failing to perform chores, actually contributes to the youngster's continuing noncompliance, which in turn irritates the mother and precipitates her violence. The mother behaves (or fails to behave) in a way that perpetuates the noncooperation problem with her older daughter. Clinicians can attend to these three interacting variables designing interventions at each level.

Abusive or neglectful families are dysfunctional to varying degrees. One or both parents may be incapacitated on a temporary or permanent basis, or be unable or simply unwilling to provide appropriate caretaking. A minority of abusive parents have severe psychiatric problems and are not amenable to therapeutic efforts; temporary or long-term placements of children may be the only solution in these cases. Some parents' ability to care for their children is so irretrievably damaged that termination of parental rights is sought and children are released for adoption.

Another way of assessing the risk of reoccurrence is by determining the severity of the abusive or neglectful behavior. One way to do this is to regard child care along a continuum (see Figure 2.1) that includes behaviors ranging from optimal care to sadistic and illegal behavior. Most parents make efforts to provide optimal care, and during periods of stress or fatigue may have episodes of inappropriate care. Inappropriate care can occur sporadically, or it may become a pattern of functioning, which creates difficulty for most young children, who need consistency and stability.

Other parents unfortunately function in the range of harmful caretaking, and sometimes the harm they inflict actually elicits attention from outsiders, causing notification of authorities. Some parents never leave physical marks on their children, and their behavior therefore is not considered illegal; yet such behavior may be sadistic, bizarre, and harmful, in spite of the fact that it may not be considered "reportable." The category to which this definition most often applies is probably situations of emotional abuse, in which children are otherwise fed, sheltered, and cared for and there are no visible injuries, but children may be placed in confined areas during waking hours, forced to exercise for long periods, shaved of all body hair, devastated by cleansing rituals, or threatened with abandonment for wrongdoing.

Most parents probably fall into the first three categories, although chronic inappropriate parenting behaviors can result in

FIGURE 2.1. Continuum of Caretaking Behavior.

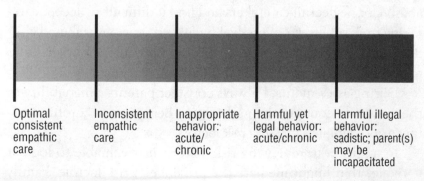

| Optimal consistent empathic care | Inconsistent empathic care | Inappropriate behavior: acute/ chronic | Harmful yet legal behavior: acute/chronic | Harmful illegal behavior: sadistic; parent(s) may be incapacitated |

harm to children and must be considered a high-risk factor. Parents who are referred for clinical services usually fall into the last two categories; they are harming their children for a variety of reasons, more or less consistently. Parents who are mandated to receive therapy have usually engaged in behavior considered illegal. They may have been referred to authorities because they have broken child abuse laws, or because a professional has concluded the children are at risk, or because the courts have imposed conditions for the children's continuation, removal, or return to their home.

In my opinion, the severity and chronicity of the abuse, coupled with the parents' willingness or unwillingness to acknowledge their problem, influence my perception of whether children can remain safely in the home or whether therapy will be most effective if children are in another, safe setting during the course of treatment.

I have had guarded success with parents whose behaviors fall into the last two categories. Success is measured by whether or not parents stop abusing or neglecting, as evidenced by a lack of subsequent referrals to the authorities. Probably the most difficult treatment scenarios are ones in which parents are apathetic, unwilling to make necessary changes, incapacitated (due to drug abuse, mental retardation, or psychiatric problems), or sadistic (they find pleasure in inflicting pain). In these cases of irretrievable damage to parents' ability to care for their children, the children must become dependents of the court, parental rights may be terminated, and the children may be released for adoption. In my experience, children always have conflictual separations from abusive or neglectful caretakers and find it difficult to accept caretaking from others. Conversely, I have seen previously abused children blossom with appropriate and consistent caretakers who patiently build secure and safe home environments.

During assessments, I always consider parents' amenability to therapy, and I consider their sabotaging behaviors or chronic resistance and denial as pressing risk factors.

In addition to reviewing risk factors, it is valuable to look at variables that might mediate the presence of risk factors. Family strengths can often counterbalance or decrease the vulnerability inherent in risk factors. Family strengths will be discussed later in this chapter.

Assessment Format

Early in treatment, clinicians must assess who their client is, who will be seen in therapy, in what order, how often, and toward what goals. These issues will be discussed in Chapter Three. Because the overall goal with families who abuse is to keep children safe by restoring appropriate parental functioning, it would appear that the client is the family; however, a special focus must remain on the children. If parents cannot keep their children out of harm's way, if they sabotage treatment, or if they are unwilling or unable to comply with social service, legal, or therapeutic recommendations, reunification efforts will be compromised or will fail despite ample coordinated efforts.

A comprehensive assessment explores individual, interactive, and systemic issues. Some family therapists prefer to see the entire family immediately to gauge family dynamics and functioning. I prefer to conduct individual assessments prior to observing interactions between family members. I believe this sequence works best for two important reasons. First, I am able to quietly interact with each individual in the family, inquire about his or her perceptions of the problem, and in doing so, establish rapport with each person. Secondly, I find it useful to compare the clients' interactions with me to their interactions with other members of the family. Differences in interaction are particularly salient with children, who tend to behave in a less guarded manner when alone with the therapist than in the presence of their parents.

Also, my view of child abuse is that it is a symptom that has emerged in the context of some level of general family dysfunction. People who mistreat, harm, injure, or ignore each other or their children are often individuals with a range of emotional, psychological, and social concerns and difficulties. One of the important goals of therapy is to restore family functioning, yet I prefer to go about this process by first attending to individuals, then to dyads, and eventually to full family interactions. An analogy that comes to mind is bowling. When the bowling pins are hit, they scatter everywhere. Although the eventual goal is to restore them to a specific order, the first step is to pick up and stabilize each one.

In order to further elucidate the assessment process, I present here an illustration of a case of physical abuse referred to me for treatment.

Clinical Case Example: The Marquez Family

Pedro Marquez had left a comfortable financial situation in which servants cared for his house and his children. His job had been threatened by his country's economic and political instability; many of his friends and colleagues had lost their professional and social positions as a result of a recent military coup and change in government. Reluctantly, he faced the fact that his future looked bleak and emigrated to the United States.

The Marquez family came to the United States in pursuit of a dream; the possibility of wealth, employment, and better education held great promise for an improved future. In particular, the promise of political freedom and physical safety seemed a panacea. Although they anticipated difficulties inherent in moving from one culture to another, they prepared by learning English and reading books that familiarized them with American customs. The preparation seemed inadequate, however, for coping with the stress of locating housing, employment, and health care, and for registering children in school, learning about public transportation, and so on.

Once in the United Sates, Mr. Marquez placed his children, Marta and Pablito, in a private Catholic school, which he paid for in advance for two years with family savings. The children seemed to like their new school. They found the priests and nuns who taught a comforting and familiar reminder of their previous school. Initially obedient and respectful, they still required a watchful eye at ages seven and nine respectively. They were quick to experiment with new dimensions of independence, for example, with expanding side trips on their long walks home.

The family's adjustment was difficult and long-term. The children did not learn English as quickly as expected, and their schoolwork suffered as a result. They were teased at school because of their dark skin and inability to communicate. The oldest child, Pablito, coped by developing a sullen and provocative manner, which teachers found disruptive. Marta tolerated her peers' ridicule better, and coped by withdrawing and becoming compliant. She quickly found another shy Latin child and they became friends and allies.

Mr. Marquez found little to spark his enthusiasm. After job hunting for months, he finally met someone who negotiated an opportunity for him to drive a cab. He took another significant portion of his earnings to buy a medallion that allowed him to drive the cab for long, continuous hours. His wife, Margarita, remained at home, caretaking for two infant neighbor children. Because she was unlicensed, she earned half of what other child-care workers earned providing the same service. She was unaccustomed to housekeeping and felt chronic fatigue. Since she had not learned to cook in her native country, she usually heated up frozen dinners for herself and her family. Everyone complained bitterly about missing their native cuisine. More often than not, the children ate breakfast and lunch at the school cafeteria, but they did not seem to like the food at school any better.

When Mr. Marquez was home, he caught up on his sleep, which frustrated Mrs. Marquez, who hoped that her husband's arrivals would offer her much-needed respite.

The Marquez family had undergone a tragic transformation. They no longer spent time together, they laughed infrequently, they were irritable with each other, and they were consumed with the constant preoccupation of making financial ends meet. There was hardly time to appreciate the inherent advantages of being in the United States: political stability and freedom.

Pablito's oppositional behavior became a serious problem in

school. He constantly fought with peers, and he griped about not fitting in or belonging. His schoolmates rejected him, which further solidified his feelings of isolation and low self-esteem. He became more and more unwilling to practice his English, because he was concerned about being ridiculed by others. He also transferred his angry mannerism to his parents, who became increasingly impatient with his defiant stance.

The first time Mr. Marquez beat Pablito was a Sunday afternoon. The youngster had been told to take his shoes off before coming into the house. As he ran in, he trailed mud all over the carpet and his mother shrieked. Mr. Marquez woke up furious, and catching a glimpse of the scene in front of him and his wife's tears, he grabbed a belt from his room and dragged Pablito into the backyard. He stripped off his pants and walloped him without restraint. Later, Mr. Marquez described this beating to child protective services in the following way: "It was no me. I get crazy, feel watch me, watch me from outside me. When I hit, I hit hard and hard, I no stop. My wife, she screams me stop. I push she away hard. I go crazy and stop, I drop belt, I stop. I held Pablito and he cry hard, blood is on his legs. I carry him inside. His mother, she take care of him. I go out and go to drinking—bar. I no believe I go crazy and hit my boy. Too many things in my mind. Too much worry. Long time I work hard, little money, long time work. No sleep."

After this first beating, Mrs. Marquez never spoke of it again. Pablito followed suit, although initially he shied away from his father. His sister Marta, however, crawled into her father's lap and hugged her dad tightly when he came home. She seemed worried about him and exhibited regressed behavior when she was in his presence. Consequently, Pablito developed antipathy toward his sister, since she seemed to get what little positive attention was available from Mr. Marquez.

Subsequent beatings followed a similar pattern. Pablito would do or say something that would infuriate his mother and Mr. Marquez would hit Pablito on behalf of his distressed wife, or perhaps as a symbolic protective gesture.

Pablito often screamed at the top of his lungs that he hated living in the States, wanted to go back home, and hated his parents for bringing him here in the first place. Clearly, he echoed everyone's sentiments about the difficulty of living in this foreign country with its different customs and demands.

Mrs. Marquez persisted in her efforts to obtain some respite when her husband arrived home. Unfortunately, Mr. Marquez had begun sleeping in his cab so that he would not lose valuable fares. When he did come home he desperately wanted to sleep more and went to any extreme to accomplish that goal, including coming home quite inebriated and passing out in bed. Mrs. Marquez kept a list of Pablito's transgressions and periodically provided the list to her husband. After the beatings occurred, Mrs. Marquez would nurse Pablito's bruises, and hold him (one of the few instances in which Pablito would allow his mother to get close to him), get both children ready for bed, and then watch television quietly, finally enjoying her coveted solitary, peaceful time.

One of the particularly brutal beatings resulted in Pablito being hit in the face by a belt buckle as he tried to turn and run away from his father's fury. A school nurse reported the facial injury to child protective services, who removed the father from the home. Then the family was referred to treatment, a process that put additional economic pressure on them. Needless to say, the family was quite resistant to therapy, and yet they eventually participated fully and successfully.

The Marquez family's story illustrates that child abuse is a problem that emerges within a family context. All members experience events that precede or precipitate abusive episodes, as well as events that follow and reinforce or perpetuate specific abusive incidents. Each person who lives in an abusive home is affected by the abuse to one degree or another. The impact of abuse is mediated by a variety of factors, including the developmental age of children, the chronicity of the abuse, how the individuals perceive and make meaning of events, and what defensive mechanisms they may employ. Denial is an effective defense, and may be classified. Trepper and Barrett (1993) catalog denial of awareness, denial of facts, denial of impact, and denial of responsibility.

Assessing Family Vulnerabilities

A comprehensive assessment includes an evaluation of vulnerabilities as well as strengths. Trepper and Barrett (1993) describe family vulnerabilities as a series of internal or external factors that make family members susceptible to stress, overwhelm their perceived abilities to cope, and weaken or overtax their abilities to resolve conflict.

In the Marquez family, several factors influenced the family's ability to function. First and foremost, their expectations and hopes were not realized by moving to the United States. Family members did not cope well with their frustrations and disappointments, retreating into separate worlds comprised of difficult work and school schedules, few rewards, feelings of isolation, increased physical labor and resulting fatigue, and for the parents, few economic gains. Ultimately, the adults begun to regard each other not as supporters but as competitors for much-needed respite time. In spite of the fact that they were a two-income family, they could not make ends meet, and their savings were exhausted during their first two years in the United States. They quickly discarded their hopes of relocating to a better neighborhood and of moving into a larger apartment.

The children continued to be unhappy and often verbalized their complaints to their parents, who were distracted, unresponsive, or overwhelmed by consistent protests. In addition, Pablito Marquez developed increasingly aggressive behavior that caused him to be identified as a problem child in school. Teachers often notified the parents of his escalating defiant behavior. The parents' most consistent response to school grievances was to put Pablito on restriction and confine him to his room. The family became more and more socially isolated. In their country, they had enjoyed a large extended family with many social interactions. Although they had some relatives in the United States, they found the distances prohibitive and transportation costly.

Probably the greatest source of stress came from the lack of positive contact between family members. An unfortunate pattern developed, in which family members no longer asked for, expected, or received physical attention, empathic care, or mutual interest. The parents had developed a pattern of inconsistent care, which escalated to periods of inappropriate and finally illegal (abusive) caretaking patterns. As the external situation continued to be frustrating, and as family members experienced feelings of despair, sadness, or anger, the distance among them grew. Unfortunately, stress in this family elicited friction and distance rather than providing momentum for feelings of unity in the face of adversity.

The physical abuse that emerged in this family was a symptom of underlying laborious family dynamics. Pablito was provocative and unruly as a result of feeling unattended and lonely. He had learned to elicit negative attention because it was the only kind of attention available to him. Eventually, he consciously or unconsciously provoked his father's pent-up rage, and the beatings became a way to relieve some of the tension in this pressure-cooker family environment.

Mr. Marquez talked in treatment about his feelings of worthlessness, acknowledging that he was a child beater and stating that this was not surprising since he felt he was generally no good. He experienced feelings of great humiliation and shame. Coming from a Latin American country in which he knew a comfortable class and position, he found it devastating to work in a subservient position. He lost his self-respect and assumed that his wife and children also held him in ill-regard. He stated that his only gratification in life was his daughter Marta, and that no matter what he did or how low he got, she always seemed to be there for him. Her unconditional love was the only thing that kept him going. He felt that he deserved little from his wife since he had uprooted her, taken her from her family, and brought her to a place in which she had to care for other people's children and to do work for which she was not prepared.

Assessing Family Strengths

Assessing family strengths allows clinicians to provide attention and support to problematic areas by utilizing the family's already-established individual and collective resources. It is often easier to identify "hot spots," or areas of potential conflict, than it is to distinguish family traits that can be viewed as functional. Clinicians must enhance their abilities to cull family strengths.

For example, when screening possible referrals and listening to the presenting problems and other pertinent information, clinicians can routinely ask for positive aspects of the family's functioning, such as how they have approached crises in the past, what they know about their family's history and obstacles that were overcome, and the traits for which individual family members are best known. If family members report significant and potentially traumatic events such as family illnesses, deaths, relocations, divorce, and so forth, I seek out information about their individual and collective coping strategies and use of resources. Some families respond positively to clinical efforts to view them as resourceful and dedicated. Families whose intentions and efforts are highlighted and relabeled as constructive even if they are not successful are more likely to view clinical efforts in a favorable light since they feel valued and fortified by clinical interactions.

A variety of factors can be considered family strengths, including a sense of humor, persistence, receptivity to others' ideas, willingness to reach out, facing problems head on, obtaining comfort and wisdom through contact with elders or religious leaders, seeking out knowledge through reading, exposing children to physical activities, making efforts to provide healthy nutrition, making time for recreational activities, helping children with homework, being interested in children's friends and activities, monitoring children's whereabouts, developing good communication skills, making efforts to feel emotionally closer, and so forth. These attitudes, abilities, intents, and behaviors can serve the clinical process well. Clinicians must allow, encourage, and motivate families to employ their strengths in the therapy process. Clinicians must convey confidence in the family and make explicit any and all efforts that are congruent with stated treatment goals. At the same time, attitudes, intents, and behaviors that sabotage must likewise be made explicit.

The Marquez family had numerous strengths which were less visible than their vulnerabilities. They were courageous, and had chosen to leave a familiar context to face less-familiar surroundings and customs. The parents had managed to save enough money to put their children in a Catholic school. The children's Catholic education was a priority and they had followed through on their commitment to the continuity of their children's religious education. Both parents had managed to find a source of income, despite the fact that their English was not perfect. As a matter of fact, the language skills of everyone in the family had improved greatly in the first year.

Both parents coped with positions for which they not been trained. Mr. Marquez had great difficulty in a service-oriented job, yet he managed to put aside his feelings to work hard and earn a living for his family. Likewise, Mrs. Marquez, who had always had caretakers for her own children, provided adequate child care to two other infant children, forging ahead in spite of the fact that she often wished she was better compensated.

The Marquez's struggled with making ends meet, yet they returned a small percentage of their income to their savings account each month. Once they had accepted the fact that they would not be able to move into a bigger apartment, they had made efforts to enhance their living environment. Mrs. Marquez had taught herself to sew by making several curtains and bedspreads that brightened up the apartment. In addition, she had slowly painted a number of rooms in the house, making attempts to lighten up an otherwise dim environment.

The family also had strengths not currently being utilized. For example, they had at one time communicated with one another openly, spent time doing family activities, and had separate hobbies and interests. Although these activities had fallen by the wayside, they had once been status quo, and as such would surely be possible to reinstate.

Their religious faith was also a strength; both parents reported the use of daily prayer, as well as taking their children to church as often as they could, although not as regularly as they had before. The parents stopped going to confession and communion on a regular basis, but insisted on their children's participation in numerous school activities.

Individual Assessment: Mr. Pedro Marquez

Pedro Marquez arrived on time and appeared fatigued and anxious. I told him that we would spend two hours together so that we would have enough time for him to provide me with whatever information about himself and his family he thought would be useful for me to know. To decrease his anxiety I told him what I had learned from child protective services and about his current situation. I said that I wanted to get some information about his childhood as well as more information about his family.

He seemed to relax as he talked about his childhood, his parents, his upbringing, his privileged status in his country, and the many warm memories of his large extended family, parties, picnics, weddings, and so forth. He spoke of his parents with great warmth and concern. He told me that without his wife's knowledge he sent a very small percentage of his salary to his parents each month. He noted that the political instability greatly compromised his family's position and that drastic changes had occurred in the last few years. For example, his parents did not have any help in the home and he worried about their ability to care for themselves in their later years.

His long-term goal was to establish residency in the United States and import his parents so he could take care of them.

He also described meeting his wife Margarita in high school. They married immediately after graduation. He got teary-eyed as he talked about her loveliness and fragility and the many plans they had made together—plans, he stated, that had disappeared in ashes. He never expected to give her what he described as "a life of hardship" and it made him "heartsick" to think that by marrying another she might have had the life she so richly deserved.

Their early marriage had been extremely happy. They were ecstatic when their son was born and looked forward to having many more children. Marta was the perfect gift, since they both fantasized about having children of each gender. Since they had come to live in the United States, his hopes of having more children were compromised by the family's situation, which he referred to as "disastrous."

Pedro had studied business after he graduated from high school and had worked for a bank for ten years. Unfortunately, military coups affected all businesses because political appointments were either removed or reinstated. Since Pedro's family was actively involved in a specific political party, changes in government compromised their livelihood and status. This instability led to his decision to come to the United States.

He then recounted his constant struggle to make ends meet in this country. He had heard that many of his countrymen had found great success here, and he was uncertain about what had led to his downfall. He talked of seeking out jobs at banks, but his lack of English seemed untenable. Employers were seeking people with bilingual capacity, and Pedro was monolingual in Spanish. His pride kept him from taking such positions as washing dishes or janitorial work, which seemed available.

When he found that he could drive a cab and work for himself, he thought he had found the perfect solution. He did not anticipate feeling so worthless in this job, and he did not realize how much money he had to pay out in rental fees and maintenance expenses.

In order to make a good return, he had to work around the clock. He often got three to four hours of sleep per night, and could not remember when he had taken a day off. As he described how hard he worked, he immediately referred to his wife's work days and how she was raising other people's children and hardly had the energy for her own. He was furious that she worked for such low pay. They both felt exploited, subservient, and fatigued.

When he talked about Pablito he was visibly sad. He said he deeply regretted beating him and that he understood why the authorities were concerned. "In a way," he confided, "I'm glad this happened, because it's given me some time to reflect on what was happening to myself and to the family." He stated that he felt out of control and took all his frustrations out on Pablito. He quickly added that Pablito was a good child, but probably too smart for his own good. He had not adjusted well to his new situation and missed his friends and extended family.

"Pablito always talks about home," Pedro said, "and I don't want to hear about it, because it just reminds me how big a mistake I made thinking I could make it here."

Pedro also spent time describing his daughter and how much he missed her since he had been away from the house. She was the only person in his life who made no demands, and seemed to offer unconditional love and affection. He felt protective of his little girl, and worried that Pablito was often rough with her.

When I inquired about his marital relationship, he seemed introspective. "There's very little there anymore." When I wondered whether he had fallen out of love with his wife, he vehemently denied that possibility. "I've been a poor excuse for a husband," he stated soberly. "I've taken her from her family and brought her to this horrible hard life." He then added, "I can't even bear to look at her anymore. I can only imagine how she must hate me." When I asked if his wife had told him this, he said that they hardly spoke to each other anymore. When I broached the subject of intimacy, he seemed embarrassed and dismissed it stating, "We have not made love for almost a year." When I asked him if this was a concern for him he said, "Sometimes, mostly not." He then discussed how busy and tired he was most of the time. "It's as if I'm being drained dry."

Lastly, I asked about violence in his background and upbringing. He stated that his parents were very easygoing people and that he was a very compliant, obedient child, "so I gave them little reason to discipline me." (He said that Pablito had also been that way before they came to the States.) His parents had never spanked him; his father would scowl and everyone obeyed. He understood his own violence in the context of his frustration and unhappiness and felt strongly that he could stop it at will. "I used to be very capable of communicating with my children," he added. "All that's gone now."

I commended Pedro on how eloquently he had communicated with me, and I remarked that he had undergone tremendous situational and personal changes when coming to this country. I told him that it was understandable that he would feel frustrated and angry, and as if he had let down his family.

"Under stress," I noted, "some families come closer and get stronger, and some families grow apart, but I've always found that families who love each other find their way back to each other." I asked him if he would be interested in learning ways to find his way back to his family, so that everyone could get and give the support and comfort they needed. He was skeptical but interested and asked when he could return for another session.

As he shook my hand good-bye, he offered a tremendous compliment: "For someone who looks so young, you've obviously learned your trade well." I knew at that point that I had established a therapeutic alliance with Mr. Marquez, in spite of some hefty obstacles such as my age, gender, and profession, and the fact that he was forced to come to see me.

Individual Assessment: Mrs. Margarita Marquez

My next task was to gain Margarita Marquez's confidence. I recognized that she also would find participation in therapy unusual and unfamiliar. She came in the following evening, and since Pedro was at work, she brought Pablito and Marta with her. I greeted them and told the children that I would be meeting with them the next day. I offered them a variety of games to use while I talked to their mother; they sat quietly and played well together in the waiting room. I showed them the office in which their mother and I would talk, and invited them to interrupt if they needed anything, which they did not do.

Margarita also appeared fatigued and nervous as we spoke. She was hesitant at first, but eventually talked freely as if she felt relieved to release her pent-up emotions.

She said she been to see a doctor when she was a child, but she remembered little about that "therapy." Her parents died in an accident when she was one year old; her elderly grandmother had raised her until she died when Margarita was eleven. She then went to live with nuns in a convent. Her great aunt was a teaching sister in the convent and she was Margarita's only living relative. When her great aunt died, Margarita had been in the convent only three months. The sisters sent her to see a counselor because they worried about how quiet she was.

Margarita continued her education in the Catholic school run by the sisters. It was during her high school years that she met Pedro Marquez at a school dance. Although several other boys had noticed her, and one of the young seminarians had kissed her, she was immediately taken with Pedro's sweet smile and happy disposition. When she visited his home, she knew that she wanted to marry him and create a family just like his: warm and content parents, lots of children, laughter, communication, and fun! Pedro's gift of language was the most appealing thing about him. "He could speak poetry at the drop of a hat. He described trips he had taken and could make foreign places come to life."

Margarita fell deeply in love with Pedro, and they were extremely complacent until the situation at home was disrupted by the Junta takeovers and many of their friends and family faced significant changes.

"He was right to come here. I don't fault him for that. Things were too unsettled in our country. Many of our friends lost everything and moved elsewhere with very little capital. We moved before we were ousted. His parents now are in difficult circumstances and I worry for them, but we talk sometimes, and they are glad we're here, offering our children a better life. Of course we don't tell them about our struggles. They believe everything is fine and that we will send for them shortly."

I asked Margarita to say more about her childhood, but she stated that she did not think about or remember that period of her life. "I can tell you that it was quiet, reserved, peaceful, but at the same time there was little fun, spontaneity, or laughter. My early life was filled with old people and rules." She added, "Lately, I've felt similar feelings to those days."

She insisted that she came to life when she met and married Pedro and was adopted by his family. "Leaving my in-laws, my family, was the hardest thing I've ever done, but I trust that someday we will be together again, either here or there." She reiterated that she maintained regular contact with her mother-in-law, and budgeting for monthly phone calls was a priority to her. She confided that Pedro did not always talk directly to his parents. "I think he feels ashamed that he hasn't been able to bring them here yet. I think he feels he's disappointing them, and it breaks his heart. He tells me what to ask them, and gives me messages for them."

When I asked her to tell me about her life since coming to the States she squeezed her handkerchief often and dried her tears. She described ongoing hardship without rest. She said the worst part was that she and her family had broken under the stress they had endured.

"I'm just as guilty as Pedro," she sobbed. "I let Pedro beat our son, partly because I wanted Pablito to stop complaining and being so angry, but partly because after the beatings, finally he was like my little boy again and I could hold him for a while. Then after everyone would sleep and it was quiet, I had some time for myself."

She asserted her love for her children and husband, as well as the pain she felt at being unable to find the strength to do for them. "I am exhausted in my soul and my heart. I feel we fight so hard, and we have so little to show for it."

When I asked her about intimacy she was self-critical: "What man would be interested? Look at me, I have so little energy to fix myself up. I am not the woman he married. I have put on weight, I have let my hair and nails go, I just don't seem to care about how I look."

Margarita clearly felt as much despair as her husband. When I mentioned to her that my job would be to help them relate to each other as a family again, she seemed interested, but as dubious as her husband. "You don't think it's too late? We seem so far apart these days." I told her that stress had a way of setting up many obstacles between people, but I was convinced that with a little assistance they could begin to find their way back to each other.

Individual Assessment: Pablito Marquez

Pablito was as visibly angry and defiant as his teachers had stated. He did not like being brought to see me, and he mistook me for someone who was keeping his father away from him. Once he understood that my job was to help the family learn to talk to each other again, and to help everyone solve the problems they had, he seemed a little less angry. His first question was whether I had seen his father and how he was. I reassured him that his father was well and eager to return home. Although at first Pablito spoke to me in English (which I perceived as a distancing technique), as he relaxed a little, he shifted to speaking to me in Spanish.

"He didn't even hit me that hard," Pablito stated. "Besides, I do bad stuff sometimes."

"Like what?" I asked.

"Like talk bad, and get in trouble in school."

"I see," I responded. "So you get in fights and yell at your mom and sister sometimes."

"Yeah." He confirmed what his parents had mentioned to me.

"Well, I agree that good kids sometimes do bad things," I said, "and I think parents need to discipline their kids."

"Yeah," Pablito asserted.

"It's just not okay for parents to beat their kids to teach them to stop doing bad things."

"But. . . ." Pablito said.

"No ifs, ands, or buts about it Pablito, your dad is a really smart guy, and he agrees with me that beating you is not the right way to correct you. He and I are going to talk about other ways to correct you and teach you that don't include beating you up." Pablito did not respond to this statement and looked away.

In the course of our visit Pablito used language sparingly, but he successfully communicated that he hated the United States, wanted to go home, missed his grandparents, cousins, and friends, and did not like anybody at school. He also confided that although Marta was okay for a girl, he did not like the way she acted "shy and sweet" just to get what she wanted from her parents.

Pablito's play reflected themes of aggression. He crashed automobiles and airplanes and sunk boats. He built tall structures and destroyed them, and he spent quite a bit of time throwing magnetic darts at the dart board. He looked over a shelf full of puppets, grabbed a scary-looking witch and yelled, "People better leave me alone or I'll cook them in boiling water."

I took the opportunity to grab a generic bear puppet and respond, "What would you do if people left you alone?"

"I would decide things just for me, and I would be rich and live in a land where everyone would be under my spell."

"And when they were under your spell, what would you make them do?"

"Just get along," he whispered, "just get along."

He took the puppet off his hand at this point and opened the door to the playroom. He walked out and said, "Okay squirt, it's your turn."

Individual Assessment: Marta Marquez

Marta was the most reserved member of the family. Her affect was compliant and quiet, not unlike how I imagined her mother had been at that age. She had few opinions and spent most of her time playing in a self-absorbed manner with the dollhouse. She spoke only when spoken to, and preferred solitary activities. After she played with the dollhouse, she sat coloring in a book, exerting considerable control over her manipulation of the crayons. Unlike many children her age who find coloring enjoyable and liberating, Marta seemed rigid and sullen as she colored.

She said she did not know why she was brought to see me. She said that she missed her daddy and hoped he would come home soon. She seemed younger than her seven years.

When I asked her point blank if she had seen daddy spank Pablito she said that she always was in her room when daddy was mad at Pablito, adding that Pablito was a "bad boy" sometimes. She noted that daddy was never mad at her and that she combed his hair and his moustache, and hugged him around the neck.

When I asked Marta about her mother she said, "Mommy takes care of little babies all the time and she's tired." I inferred that Marta was sad that her mother had little time for her, a fact that her mother herself had volunteered.

In Marta's dollhouse play she had repeatedly put the mother doll in the little girl's room and had the mother combing the little girl's hair and rocking her in a chair. Usually Marta placed little babies "downstairs" covered up with Kleenex. They made no noises and they were kept from mother's view. Most importantly, the mother in Marta's play chose to spend all her time with her own little girl.

Although Pablito seemed to mirror the frustration, anger, and disappointment in the family, Marta seemed to mirror the depression and avoidance.

Couple Assessment: Margarita and Pedro Marquez

Margarita and Pedro Marquez arrived forty-five minutes late, symbolically recreating what each stated their primary concern was: a lack of time for each other and their children. Pedro was late because he had a fare that took longer than anticipated, and Margarita was late because she had to wait for her next-door neighbor to watch the children.

The couple had not seen each other for a few weeks and they greeted each other with a kiss on the cheek and a pat on the back. They both looked sadder than either had looked alone.

I told them I was aware that it was awkward for them to have their first meeting in my presence and I thought they might want to take some time and ask each other any questions they wished. They spoke to each other quietly about how they were doing, each reassuring the other that things were not as bad as they could be.

I then reiterated my understanding that our therapy was to address the issue of physical abuse, and that to do that we would spend time addressing the problems in the family that had led to Pedro's aggression. I then asked them to say a few words about what they each thought contributed to their problems.

Pedro spoke first and suddenly burst into tears, asking his wife's forgiveness for causing them such problems. He listed a range of concerns including making the mistake of leaving their country, how he did not blame her for not respecting him any longer, how it broke his heart to see her having to work taking care of other people's children. He further stated that he felt burdened by his feelings of failure and would not blame her if she wanted to leave him.

Mrs. Marquez allowed her tears to fall freely as she listened to her husband, and finally she said, "Where would I go? My place is with you. Our place is together." She went on to reassure him that he had made the right choice, that she knew it was hard but they were doing alright. She reminded him that their mission now was to create a better life for the children, a life that was not available back in their country.

I waited as they sat together without touching, and interjected that their goal was honorable, that their children's future was important to all parents. I then stated the obvious: "Part of preparing them for the future is providing them with love and comfort and security today. It's important to work and give them a roof over their heads, but it's equally important for them to have a warm and happy environment."

We spent the rest of this first joint meeting clarifying the potential goals of future treatment. I proposed a treatment plan that included individual therapy for Pedro, couples therapy, and conjoint family sessions. Since I had already committed to being the family's therapist, I offered them a sliding-scale fee, and they were most appreciative. I defined the couples and family work as the most relevant, since the family was in crisis and child abuse was the symptom of that distress.

Family Assessment: The Marquez Family

The children were visibly nervous as they waited for their father to arrive for the family meeting. Pablito kept asking what time it was and Marta kept crawling in and out of her mother's lap. Pedro arrived ten minutes late and the children ran into his arms. He caressed them and held them close for a few minutes and commented on Pablito's new sweater and Marta's barrette. Margarita cried as she watched the warm reunion, commenting to me in a later session how rare it was to see her husband and children greet each other in a warmhearted way.

Pedro sat on the couch holding Marta. Pablito sat opposite him, focused on his every word. The following conversation ensued:

THERAPIST: Well, it's been a while since you've all been together. Anybody got any questions?

MARTA: Daddy, when are you coming home?

FATHER: I don't know, my child, I hope it's very, very soon.

MARTA: Where are you sleeping?

FATHER: Over at Miguel's house. You remember Miguel, he drives a cab too.

MARTA: I miss you and want you to come home.

FATHER: I miss you too, my daughter, and I promise I'm going to work hard to get back home to you soon.

THERAPIST: Do you have any questions, Pablito?

PABLITO: No.

THERAPIST: Are you sure?

PABLITO: I don't have any questions.

THERAPIST: Okay, maybe your dad has something to say.

FATHER: Pablito, I want you to know that I am sorry for hitting you and hurting you.

PABLITO: It's OK, Daddy, I don't care.

FATHER: I care. I was wrong. There were so many things going on, my son, and I was frustrated, and I felt that I had let you and your sister and mother down. We came here with so many dreams and now we have all been unhappy.

PABLITO: It's not so bad, Dad.

FATHER: Well, it's not as good as what I wanted for you.

PABLITO: Then why can't we go home, Dad? Why can't we go back to Grandma's and Grandpa's?

FATHER: I know, my son, but there's much you don't understand. The situation back home is not good for us now. Things will never be the same for us again. There's too much instability. Suddenly you can lose everything.

PABLITO: But we've lost everything already.

FATHER: I know it feels that way, but your mother and I and the doctor have spoken, and the truth is that as long as we have each other, we will be fine. But we have to get to know each other again, we have to learn to trust each other.

THERAPIST: And I think one of the things that's important is for everyone to be honest about, and begin to communicate, their feelings to one another. I think people have been hiding their feelings from each other.

MOTHER: I agree with that.

THERAPIST: As an example, has anybody been feeling lonely?

MOTHER: I have.

MARTA: And I feel sad when Mommy has to take care of the babies.

THERAPIST: And you, Pablito?

PABLITO: I don't care about that.

THERAPIST: What do you care about?

PABLITO: I don't.

FATHER: Son, don't be disrespectful. The doctor is asking you a question. Answer her properly.

PABLITO: I just don't know, really.

I went over to the puppet shelf, grabbed the witch puppet, and brought it over to Pablito.

THERAPIST: Here, Pablito, maybe the witch can tell me more.

MOTHER: Oh my goodness, that looks like a scary witch.

PABLITO: It's not a she. It's a mad witch, rrrrgggggggg.

THERAPIST: Tell your dad what you're mad about, Mr. Witch.

PABLITO: Everything. The world. The aliens coming to invade. The jerks that bother me, everything.

THERAPIST: Tell Pedro, Mr. Witch.

PABLITO: And you aren't ever there to help us. You are a traitor to the people. You bring us. . . .

THERAPIST: Go on.

PABLITO: I don't want to do this anymore [removing witch puppet from hand].

MOTHER: That was good what you did, my boy. I feel that

way too, like Pedro isn't around to help us much anymore. And I feel lost, and frightened, and I don't feel comfortable in this country with people who don't understand me, and people who I can't understand.

MARTA: [*Holding a puppy dog puppet*] Rugh, rugh. Mommy, look, I want a puppy like this.

PABLITO: Shut up, dummy. You know we can't have a dog because they won't let us have one in the apartment.

FATHER: Pablito, don't call your sister dumb. She's a little girl, she doesn't know any better.

PABLITO: But mom was talking, then she had to talk about the stupid dog.

THERAPIST: So you thought what your mom was saying was important.

PABLITO: Yes.

THERAPIST: Margarita, what else would you like to tell your family?

MOTHER: [*Sobbing*] I just feel like I've been a bad mother. I've been so tired, I haven't paid attention to either of you . . . any of you . . . the way I wished.

THERAPIST: Mr. Marquez, any comments?

FATHER: Children, your mother and I both feel this way. She feels unhappy that she has to work and that working keeps her tired and she doesn't have enough time for you. We have all had a hard time.

PABLITO: But you never say that dad, you always talk about how you like it here.

FATHER: I haven't been truthful with you Pablito, and besides, you complain all the time, so I try to show you the positives.

THERAPIST: Tell Pablito what it's been like for you.

FATHER: Oh, my son, if only I could explain to you how it's been. It's been . . . well . . . the hardest time of my life. I feel mortified working as a cabdriver, having to be polite to rude people who treat me as if I was not a person. And all the while I worry for you and your problems at school, and about your mother, your beautiful mother, who never worked a day in her life before we moved here, having to wash and scrub and cook. And I feel that no matter what I do I just can't win.

PABLITO: Why don't you kick their butts, Dad?

FATHER: What? What are you talking about?

PABLITO: The people that get in the cab who are rude and disrespect you, why don't you just lock the doors and beat their butts, teach them a lesson?

FATHER: Violence is not the answer to anything, Pablito, not with rude people, and not with you, my son. Part of being a man is learning to work out your problems without resorting to violence. I have believed that all my life, and I'm sorry I ever laid a finger on you. Feeling angry at ignorant people is okay, but we have to learn to accept our feelings and not behave in ways that later shame us. This is one of the reasons we are coming to see Dr. Gil, so that I can learn to deal better with my anger, and you also, Pablito.

This family session was poignant in many respects. As family members developed comfort in sharing their feelings and in listening and responding to each other, some of the barriers of distance and resentment began to dissipate.

Additional Assessment Considerations

A helpful way of assessing family interactions is to ascertain the type of family interactions the family uses most, and the extent to which these interactions prevail.

All families engage in three distinctive types of interactions: positive, negative, or neutral. *Positive interactions* feel rewarding to those involved and promote understanding and emotional connectedness. *Negative interactions* include verbal hostility, unresolved conflicts, and irritable or curt communications, which create emotional distance. *Neutral interactions* also create emotional distance, not as a result of negative contacts, but because there is a paucity of empathic care, interest, communication, and rewarding exchanges.

Figure 2.2 illustrates the Marquez family's types and levels of interaction. The predominant type of contact is negative, as evidenced by parental violence. The second most prominent type is neutral, since family members rarely spend time together, engage in activities together, or communicate with one another. A certain amount of positive interactions occur when the parents physically nurture or comfort their children; Pablito allows himself to be nurtured by his mother after beatings, and Marta has developed a

FIGURE 2.2. Types of Interaction in the Marquez Family.

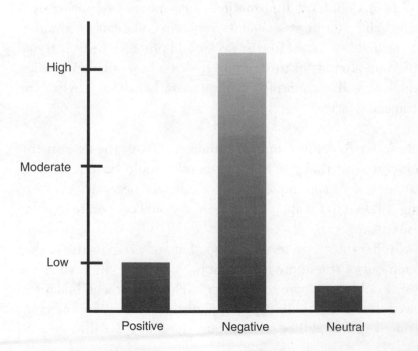

pattern of comforting father in order to keep family peace, and perhaps to keep herself from becoming the target of his angry outbursts.

Assessing types and levels of family interactions allows me to devise treatment strategies to increase the number of positive interactions, decrease negative ones, and stabilize the presence of neutral interactions, which are not necessarily negative if balanced by a range of interactions.

Environmental Factors.   A family assessment also reviews environmental factors as part of the risk factors. In the case of the Marquez family, my home visit revealed a clean and organized environment within a low-income housing project that enjoyed reasonable security. Since the children had after-school activities, they spent little time playing in the neighborhood streets. Margarita and Pedro had insisted from the outset that the children's friends visit them in their home.

Review of Collateral Information.   As mentioned earlier, it is always helpful during assessments to obtain collateral information from available sources. In this case, child protective services had written up a report of the initial physical abuse incident, which Pedro had readily confirmed, adding to, rather than denying, the documented facts.

Criteria for Accepting into Treatment.   After the assessment, I felt confident that the Marquez family would be amenable to treatment, would attend sessions, would make necessary efforts to bring children in for appointments, and would cooperate in every possible way.

Child protective services had demanded that the father remain out of the home for six months, during which time the family would participate in treatment. The worker who had interviewed the family did not speak Spanish and was therefore compromised in her ability to ascertain the family's willingness to acknowledge the problem and develop nonphysical ways of disciplining the children.

Special Needs and Referral Options. During assessments, I make note of any special needs that might necessitate referrals to community resources or adjunct services. On occasion, I have accepted families into treatment with the understanding that they take part in adjunct services such as drug treatment or use specialized services such as respite care, self-help groups, or crisis services.

Cross-Cultural Considerations. When working across cultures, it is important to familiarize oneself with basic information about a client's cultural background. Although some of this information can be obtained by asking clients to provide information, to rely on clients can be perceived as burdensome or intrusive.

Working with the Marquez family, I drew on my own personal experience as someone whose family emigrated to the United States. My background allowed me to understand some of the difficulties of cultural transitions; yet it was important for me to learn about this particular family's political, religious, and social status in order to further comprehend their current difficulties.

The family was very relieved to be able to use their first language in therapy. They complained bitterly about the strain of making themselves understood in a foreign language. Likewise, they were satisfied with my ability to validate the culture shock they had experienced, and the ways in which they continued to miss their homeland in spite of the fact that political instability prohibited their return.

Both Pedro and Margarita Marquez emphasized how important it was to them that someone understood the status transformation they had undergone and the challenge of remaining optimistic when their self-image had been altered.

Assessment Instruments. A number of assessment instruments are available that may be useful in assessing parental attitudes and behaviors toward their children. At the end of the book is a list of assessment instruments that I have found particularly helpful.

Formulation of the Problem

Pedro and Margarita Marquez both needed help with their feelings of worthlessness and despair. Their positive interactions had decreased, and negative interactions increased; their primary mode of interaction was neutral. They ignored each other and led separate lives. Their neutral stance was perceived as lack of empathic care, interest, and concern. Consequently, the parents were unhappy with each other, and this affected their ability to provide adequate or nurturing parenting. As their ability to parent in a warm, supportive, affectionate way became compromised, the children's behavior was exacerbated. Pablito developed an offensive posture in order to get his attention needs met; Marta developed caretaking skills that guaranteed positive attention from her father.

Although the children's adaptive strategies were helpful to them, there were consequences to their behaviors. Pablito's acting-out behavior created a difficult situation for the parents in that they were frequently called by the school about their son's behavior. They perceived these phone calls as further evidence of their failure. That is, they could not control their son in the same way that they felt they could not control their own destiny. They felt shame and low self-esteem, which then contributed to resentment of their son, who they saw as a source of aggravation.

The parents treated each child differentially. Pablito received negative attention, and Marta learned to be compliant and affectionate in order to get her needs met and stay safe. Her caretaking behavior toward her father expressed her preoccupation with his volatile behavior, as well as her desire for nurturing contact with the parent she perceived as more accessible.

Marta and Pablito had grown distant from each other. Pablito became jealous of the positive attention Marta received from her father. His aggressive behavior toward her increased, which also provoked violent responses from their father. Marta viewed Pablito as the bad child who provoked her father's wrath. Neither mother nor brother were perceived as sources of affection or consistent love to Marta.

The abuse was usually followed by periods of respite for all family members. The beatings released negative pent-up emotions such as frustration, helplessness, and despair. After the beatings, both parents nurtured the children (the mother nurtured Pablito, the father nurtured Marta) and asked their forgiveness. A pattern developed in which the beatings were followed by what the children perceived as a positive outcome. It may be that Pablito's provocative behavior was fueled by the knowledge that violence led to nurturance, or proof of love, which had become elusive in this home.

Everyone in the family played a role that maintained an ongoing pattern of tension building, tension release, and affection, a pattern aptly described by Walker (1979) in families in which spouse abuse occurs.

One hundred percent of the responsibility for the abuse is with the person who abuses, who must be accountable for his or her unacceptable behavior. Margarita Marquez allowed the abuse to continue unabated, however, and therefore failed to protect her children or allowed them to be placed in harm's way. Sometimes, she recounted the son's wrongdoing, knowing that a violent outburst would be provoked. However, violent episodes were followed by peaceful time alone, which motivated her to minimize or deny the impact of the beatings.

Lastly, Marta was frightened and concerned for her father, and she took great pains to soothe and comfort him in an effort to stay safe and get positive self-regard for her caretaking skills.

The family underwent further crisis when the father was prohibited from staying in the home. Pablito felt guilty that his father had been sent away, and he felt responsible for the beatings. Marta felt more depressed when her father was no longer available to her, and spent most of her time alone in her room. Margarita sunk into a deep depression reminiscent of a period of time in her youth when she was joyless and alone. Everyone was worried for Pedro, who was desperate to return home and begin a reparative process. Time away from home and the impending threat of imposed family separation ignited a retrospective period in which Pedro bemoaned his role in the family's breakdown.

Obviously, this heightened period of despair was paradoxically the time of greatest receptivity in the family, since crisis equals opportunity. I reassured each family member that my goal was to help everyone feel more content, get emotionally closer to each other, and deal with their problems in more appropriate ways.

This assessment revealed a family who was receptive to help, eager to reconnect with each other, willing to discard violent behaviors, and willing to explore and utilize new coping strategies. During treatment, great progress was made, partly because there was a tradition of family cohesion and respect. Pedro Marquez returned to the family within six months and continued in therapy for three months after reunification. The family wrote me from time to time, and it was clear that the crisis had allowed them to reevaluate their situation and make better choices reflective of their mutual love and concern.

Pedro never hit Pablito again, and served as a role model for his son's aggressive tendencies. The sibling relationship became less conflictual as the parents became more available to both children and they no longer had to compete for limited parental attention.

How Assessment Guides Treatment Planning

The above assessment had been sequenced so that individual meetings preceded couples, parent-child, and family sessions. Likewise, therapy was provided to both parents individually, then to the children separately and together, to the couple, and finally to the entire family unit.

Both parents had acute individual needs and responded well to receiving focused clinical attention. As each began to feel better about himself or herself, they seemed to find motivation to redirect efforts toward emotional contact with each other. As they became more securely defined as a couple, as parents they interacted in a healthier way with the children both individually and collectively.

Although there are no rigid guidelines about working systemically—on occasion I have worked systemically through one available family member—careful consideration must be given to strengthening a foundation on which other family bridges can be built.

As the name implies, a family assessment evaluates individual and family functioning, determining family vulnerabilities and strengths, risk factors, and precipitating stressors. It is helpful to assess child abuse along a continuum of parental caretaking, acknowledging parental incapacitation or apathy which hinders children's safety. In addition, calculating types and levels of interactions may allow clinicians to develop appropriate interventions. Finally, the assessment process creates ample opportunities to establish therapeutic alliances with all family members, which in turn increases the family's receptivity to proposed treatment plans.

3

Principles of Treatment

Abusive behavior must be confronted openly and precisely. Over the years, I have experimented with many ways of doing this, and I will share the approaches I have found most useful.

Making Abusive or Neglectful Behaviors Ego-Dystonic

Once parents become more receptive to clinical interventions, clinicians proceed by discussing some of the problem behaviors that precipitated the referral. If parents are still in denial, the discussion becomes generic rather than specific.

Denial is characteristic of parents who abuse and neglect, and it can be viewed as protective behavior that will remain in place until families feel they do not need to guard themselves or their situations as closely as they had been. In other words, denial precedes the formation of trust and does not have to represent a significant obstacle early in treatment.

In the following example, I take a generic approach with a mother who denies wrongdoing and then proceed to discuss the various ways in which (alleged or hypothetical) situations may be more or less appropriate or safe. Child protective services had been called by concerned teachers after they learned that Tyrone was unattended late into the night. They had observed his lethargic and distracted behavior in school, which might have resulted from sleep deprivation. In addition, the teachers concurred that Tyrone's schoolwork had deteriorated.

> THERAPIST: I talked with child protective services this morning and the worker is concerned about Tyrone missing too much school, and about the fact that teachers have noticed him hoarding food at school and daydreaming. His teacher says he is distracted and tired all of a sudden, and although Tyrone hasn't said anything specific, they worry that he might be alone too much.
>
> MOTHER: First of all, I never leave my son alone without good reason. I have to go to work and support me and Tyrone, and sometimes I can't find child care. He is eight years old, old enough to be alone and take care of himself for short times. Lots of his friends are alone—I don't know why they're not out investigating everybody in my complex.
>
> THERAPIST: So you feel as though you've been singled out.
>
> MOTHER: Darn tooting. If my cheeks were rosy pink like that worker's, no way she would be picking on me.
>
> THERAPIST: You feel that you've been investigated because you're Black.
>
> MOTHER: Yes ma'am I do. No way I would be in this kind of trouble if I wasn't black.
>
> THERAPIST: To tell you the truth, I do think that people from different ethnic groups seem to be identified and referred to authorities more often.
>
> MOTHER: I know that.
>
> THERAPIST: And I'm very sensitive to that issue. I didn't pick anything up from the worker so far, but I want you to know

that I agree with you that Blacks and Latins and Asians are often referred more quickly. What's it like for you to see a White therapist?

MOTHER: To be honest with you, I didn't expect anything different.

THERAPIST: So you assumed I would be White.

MOTHER: Yeap.

THERAPIST: And you don't have any feelings about that?

MOTHER: I didn't say that. I just said that I didn't expect you to be anything other than white. I've been down this road before.

THERAPIST: You've been in therapy before?

MOTHER: Look, can you just tell me what's gonna happen now, and how long I have to come here?

THERAPIST: Well, I first need to understand what the problems are, so I need to ask a few more questions. For example, you said that you never leave him alone, except when there's a good reason. Can you give me an example of a good reason?

MOTHER: I'm supporting this kid by myself. I finally got off the welfare roles three years ago and since then I've been working like a dog.

THERAPIST: What kind of work do you do?

MOTHER: Whatever I can. I got trained as a pipe fitter, but it's hard to get steady work in that area . . . lots of layoffs, and I'm the first to go 'cause I don't have seniority anyplace.

THERAPIST: Good for you, completing that training. I hear it's tough for women to get jobs in that field.

MOTHER: Not for me. The only problem I had was keeping the jobs I got.

THERAPIST: What other work do you do?

MOTHER: I do whatever I can, whenever I can. Mostly, I can do waitressing work, and a friend of mine works in a farmer's market, so sometimes I go help her sell. I sell stuff at flea markets, too. I got lots of junk I sell for other people.

THERAPIST: Wow, it sounds like you work a lot.

MOTHER: Yeah, I do.

THERAPIST: So do you sometimes leave Tyrone alone when you're working?

MOTHER: When I got to go, I got to go. Let's say my friend calls me at 11:00 and she says get your butt down here, so and so didn't show up, I gotta get there quick or she'll find someone else.

THERAPIST: And Tyrone's already in school?

MOTHER: Yeah. So he's cool. He knows I gotta work so we can live. He doesn't complain. He likes to be home alone.

THERAPIST: And how long is he alone?

MOTHER: Well, sometimes if things are going pretty good I might stay at the flea market till it closes at 9:00.

THERAPIST: So he's home from let's say 2:30 until 9:00.

MOTHER: Yeah, but only when stuff comes up.

THERAPIST: Do you worry about him?

MOTHER: Nah. He's fine alone. The only problem is that he doesn't always do his homework . . . he watches too much TV.

THERAPIST: Oh, so there's a down side to his being home alone. Too much TV, not enough homework.

MOTHER: Yeah.

THERAPIST: Anything else?

MOTHER: He sometimes stays up too late and he falls asleep on the couch. When I get home I wake him up and if he hasn't done his homework I make him do it, no matter what time it is.

THERAPIST: What's the latest you ever get home?

MOTHER: Well, sometimes it takes time to load my friend's truck and all, so sometimes it can get later . . . like midnight.

THERAPIST: Oh, so sometimes he's home alone for longer than six hours.

MOTHER: Yeah but I told you, he's a good kid, he doesn't get into any trouble, he pretty much stays to himself because when I'm not home he's not allowed to have friends over.

THERAPIST: Has he ever done that anyway?

MOTHER: A couple of times, but he knows better now.

THERAPIST: Uh huh, I see. It sounds like you have a lot of stuff going on in your life: no steady job, a kid to raise by yourself. By the way, does Tyrone see his dad at all?

MOTHER: No. He didn't want anything to do with a kid. He split when he knew I was pregnant.

THERAPIST: So you're raising him alone, you have a good trade, but you can't always keep those jobs you're trained for, and you got some friends helping you out but sometimes that means being ready to go at a moment's notice and Tyrone ends up staying home alone.

MOTHER: Yeah, that's pretty much it.

THERAPIST: What about the other things that the teachers are saying, about Tyrone hoarding food, and being distracted in class?

MOTHER: That's the first I've heard of it. They never called to tell me anything about that. And his teacher goes to the same church I do. I saw her in church last week and she didn't say anything about Tyrone, problems with Tyrone.

THERAPIST: Well, that's interesting. I wonder just what they mean by "distracted"?

MOTHER: I don't know. But I do know that Tyrone's been stealing food since he was six years old and found out he could get away with it.

THERAPIST: Why does he do it?

MOTHER: Wouldn't you? If you could? I don't buy none of that junk that kids like these days, so he's always begging people for junky stuff. Then they made fun of him so he just started snatching it.

THERAPIST: What does he like besides junk food?

MOTHER: He loves ribs, hot dogs, hamburgers, potatoes, you know, stuff most kids eat. But he's also lazy. Doesn't like to cook for himself, likes it better when I'm home and I make dinner—beans and wieners, he loves those cans, but he has a hard time opening them when I'm not home.

THERAPIST: Sounds like he misses you.

MOTHER: Or he likes to get waited on hand and foot.

THERAPIST: Oh, you've spoiled him have you?

MOTHER: Not lately. But sometimes I baby him. I felt guilty that he didn't have a dad, didn't want him to miss out on stuff.

THERAPIST: So how often would you say you have dinner together now?

MOTHER: Ooo, I can't remember the last time . . . months at least.

THERAPIST: Do you miss being home for dinner?

MOTHER: Yeah, sometimes, especially 'cause sometimes the food they have at the markets is boring, you keep wanting some hot food, maybe something that's not fried in a ton of fat.

THERAPIST: Hum. Well, I tell you what. I think you're doing a heck of a job and trying really hard here for your kid. I know that it would be better for Tyrone to have someone to watch him, just because he's eight, and eight-year-olds can watch too much TV or not do their home-work.

MOTHER: Do you know how much baby-sitters charge these days? And most of them don't do anything but watch TV themselves.

THERAPIST: Pretty expensive, huh?

MOTHER: Yeah. And there not always around when you need them, or if you need them right away.

THERAPIST: Does the school have an after-school program?

MOTHER: That was my first thought, but if he goes there I gotta pick him up at the same time each day, and my schedule doesn't work like that.

THERAPIST: That makes it complicated. But do you know if there's room for him in after-school care?

MOTHER: I got no idea at this point.

THERAPIST: Okay. Well, I'm gonna see if I can be helpful to you here. One thing I hear you say is that you do worry about Tyrone when he's alone because he doesn't go to sleep on time, doesn't eat well, and doesn't do his home-work. But trying to find someone who can be around at a moment's notice is hard. Let me ask you another question. Tyrone aside, how do you feel about kids staying at home alone for more than say, two hours at a time?

MOTHER: I don't even watch the TV anymore, it scares me to see what's going on out there.

THERAPIST: What do you mean?

MOTHER: The child-snatching, the perverts, the drugs being sold to kids on the street, all that stuff is scary. And when I hear the news, it's usually kids Tyrone's age. It's crazy what goes on.

THERAPIST: So generally speaking, you think kids are less safe now than before.

MOTHER: No question.

THERAPIST: Okay, so there's even another reason to figure out how to get him supervised while you do what you need to earn a living.

MOTHER: Good luck.

THERAPIST: Well, luck and then some. I'll have to talk to the worker, and by the way, I will need to check in with the school to see how he's doing.

MOTHER: Yeah, tell them to remember who his mother is, and that they should talk to me first if they got some kind of concern about Tyrone.

THERAPIST: Well, you might want to tell them that directly, but I'll definitely try to get a sense of what their concerns are. I'd like to see Tyrone tomorrow at about four, if that's okay with you, and then you and I can meet next week. That should give me time to get some more answers.

MOTHER: Okay. What do you want me to tell Tyrone about coming here? He already freaked about that worker coming to talk to him at school.

THERAPIST: Just tell him that I'm a counselor who talks to kids and I just want to meet him and get to know him a little. Tell him I won't ask a lot of questions, he can tell me whatever he wants, and there's lots of good toys to play with in the playroom.

This mother seemed concerned for her son and overwhelmed by the demands of having to take whatever work comes along. Her efforts to obtain child care had been unsuccessful and she had developed a pattern of leaving Tyrone alone whenever work became available. Because she felt helpless to secure child care for Tyrone, she had convinced herself that he was fine while she was away. Her initial defensiveness gave way to her trusting me with realistic worries not only about what Tyrone did when he was home alone but about what could happen to him in an unstable and dangerous world.

This mother had tremendous strengths and sincerely loved her child and struggled for their survival. I talked to the worker about creating a supportive environment that included after-school care as well as financial support for baby-sitting. The social worker was able to access a funding source that provided the mother with financial assistance. I worked with the mother on setting up a structure in which there were at least three baby-sitters she could call, including two that had the ability to pick up Tyrone after school. The mother located an adult female baby-sitter who already picked up a friend of Tyrone's from school and took the child to her house for daily child care.

The mother promised the social worker that she would make the necessary phone calls to arrange for Tyrone to be picked up from school when she had to go to work. The baby-sitter allowed the mother to pick Tyrone up from her home whenever she was finished working. Once the baby-sitting problem was resolved, Tyrone returned to a normal routine and his schoolwork improved immediately. The mother was in therapy for three months, during which time she discussed her personal and career goals.

I think the case proceeded as well as it did because the mother's defensiveness was diffused early on. I focused on what she did not like about her child being alone rather than arguing about why children needed to be supervised. Once she confronted her own denial (that is, she actually did prefer that he be supervised), she was able to accept available help. I quickly mobilized the system to allow her access to after-school care that was available through child protective services. The mother was very grateful for the funding provided for child care and recognized the stipend as a symbol of concrete help. She then felt empowered to pursue baby-sitting options and secured a caretaker who met her needs perfectly.

My interviews with Tyrone revealed a child who was confident and content. He interacted well with adults as well as with peers.

His mother was a source of nurturing and support to him and he confided how much he missed her and worried about her when she was gone. He also proudly admitted that when she was home she helped him with his homework and could explain things better than his teacher.

He complained that he couldn't play with his friends after school and let slip that sometimes he snuck out for a little while without his mother knowing.

When I asked what his specific worries were about his mother he said that she worked too hard, did not get enough to eat, and was tired all the time. I remarked how Tyrone and his mom had exactly the same worries about each other and he laughed.

Although this child's initial symptoms provoked suspicions in his teachers, and although it is almost always safer to supervise young children, Tyrone was not abused or emotionally neglected in the classic sense. It was not parental apathy that created a problem situation, it was the parent's response to feeling stressed, over-whelmed, and worried about her child, as well as the pressure she felt to take whatever paying jobs came her way. This pressure over-rode her reservations about leaving Tyrone alone. Clinical inter-ventions focused on decreasing her resistance, on encouraging her to recognize that leaving Tyrone unsupervised was ego-dystonic to her, on accessing resources, and on helping her set up a structure for both working when she could and ensuring that Tyrone was super-vised when she did work.

Teaching Alternative Behaviors

The most ineffectual and dangerous clinical intervention is to tell parents that they must stop the abuse or neglect behaviors without equipping them with an effective alternative behavior. Parents who physically hurt their children may be trying to discipline them, may lack education about childrearing, may be impulsive, frustrated, or controlling, or may be inadvertently repeating the parenting behav-iors of their own parents.

Alternatives to Physical Abuse

Physically abusive parents need to learn that violence is not a solution to their problems. They need to learn disciplinary techniques that respect children's developmental capacities, elicit cooperation, and shape children's behavior in a nonhurtful way.

Clinicians who work with families in which physical abuse has taken place must equip themselves with knowledge about disciplinary strategies, and must be able to demonstrate how techniques can be applied to specific behaviors that elicit parental concern. To do so, clinicians must first assist parents to describe the behaviors that cause them difficulty, to list prior attempts to solve their problems, to accept and incorporate alternative parenting behaviors, and to rehearse these appropriate behaviors so they can achieve their goals in an efficient manner.

In the following example, I first form an alliance with the parents by empathizing with them and their problem. I then have them report what about their child's behavior is upsetting, what they have tried, and what works the best, and then give them ideas for other techniques they might attempt.

> THERAPIST: I know exactly what you mean. I found it really annoying when my kids sassed back at me.
>
> FATHER: I'm not sure you're getting the full picture. We're not talking about "sassing." This kid is out of control. He hollers at us in a defiant, even threatening way, and he uses words even I don't use with regularity, and he gets right in our faces. It's like watching him come unglued.
>
> THERAPIST: I see.
>
> MOTHER: And since he's turned twelve he's grown about two feet and he actually towers over me, and I don't even recognize him when he's like that, and I think he could really hurt me.
>
> THERAPIST: That sounds really frightening. Let's talk about the recent incident.

FATHER: That's easy. I punched his lights out and it was the best thing I ever did. I don't care what you people say. This kid needs someone to knock some sense into him.

THERAPIST: Let's start there. The incident that precipitated the child abuse report. First of all, how did the report get made?

MOTHER: He had a black eye and the teacher asked him what happened to him.

FATHER: So he acted like a little victim and said his father had hit him. Of course he didn't say anything about what he did, he just gave the teacher the impression that his out-of-control father had lost it.

THERAPIST: So he gave the teacher half the story, the half about being hit.

FATHER: That's right. It makes me boil thinking about the damn kid accusing me of abusing him, for Christ's sake.

THERAPIST: The teacher hadn't heard your half of the story, about how worried you've been about Jasper.

MOTHER: We're really concerned about what's going on with him—he seems so angry all the time.

THERAPIST: Any idea what he's so angry about?

MOTHER: You know, we've talked about that a lot. This all started when we started setting limits on him, you know, curfews and stuff. He really rebelled after we told him that he couldn't be out until all hours of the night.

THERAPIST: So the trouble you've had with him is recent.

FATHER: I would say in the last year and a half or so.

THERAPIST: Any other major changes during that time?

MOTHER: We moved. Jasper didn't want to move, you know how kids are, we just figured he'd get over it.

THERAPIST: Has he?

MOTHER: Well, we thought so, but now I don't know.

THERAPIST: Have you asked him about it?

MOTHER: Well, we just don't go up and ask him stuff, we have to wait until he's in a talking mood and then we can ask him a few things, but he shuts down real quick.

THERAPIST: He sounds a little moody and quiet.

FATHER: Yeah, he's quiet, until he screams and yells at us like a crazy loon.

THERAPIST: What kinds of things have you tried in the past to get him to stop yelling?

MOTHER: At first we would take away his TV privileges. That worked for a while, and then he said he didn't care.

THERAPIST: What else?

FATHER: I wouldn't let him go out during the weekend and he had to do extra chores.

THERAPIST: Okay. So you took away privileges and gave him extra chores, anything else?

MOTHER: Not that I can remember. Jim, anything else?

FATHER: Nope. Nothing seemed to work.

THERAPIST: How often were these screaming episodes happening?

FATHER: Once a week or so.

THERAPIST: That often huh?

FATHER: Well, I guess it feels that way, I'm not so sure, maybe I'm exaggerating.

MOTHER: Yeah, I think it felt like we were fighting all the time.

THERAPIST: What was it like between you and your son, Mr. S., when you weren't in a shouting match?

FATHER: Jasper and I got along great when he was smaller.

THERAPIST: Yeah, what was it like?

FATHER: We used to spend lots of weekend time together. I'd try to give Sal a break, so she could do things she couldn't do during the week. I looked forward to spending time with Jasper.

THERAPIST: What kind of things did you do?

FATHER: We went fishing, camping mostly. Sal never liked going out in the wild. Jasper took to it right from the start.

THERAPIST: When was the last time you went?

FATHER: About two years ago, a little before we moved. I got a new job, a promotion really, and I had a lot of work to do during the weekend.

MOTHER: I think he really misses those outings.

FATHER: Oh, yeah, I can just see it now. We'd probably kill each other out there in the wilderness. They'd have to come looking for our bodies.

THERAPIST: You feel really pessimistic about your chances with your son right now.

FATHER: It's been pretty miserable lately.

THERAPIST: How about you, Mrs. S.? What was it like for you and your son when you weren't in shouting matches?

MOTHER: Well, we always got along . . . not like his dad and him, but we were close and we always felt easy with each other. It was different than with his dad. We did homework together, watched television, mostly sports, and I drove him to his sports activities, which he doesn't do anymore either by the way, and then we always went shopping together and to the movies. He and I liked going to the movies a lot.

THERAPIST: So you also had a comfortable relationship with him.

MOTHER: That would be the best description.

THERAPIST: So, it sounds like we need to figure out how to diffuse the anger that's built up.

FATHER: Well, when I socked him out it got his attention.

THERAPIST: How did you feel after you realized you had hit him hard enough to give him a black eye?

FATHER: Honestly, I had mixed feelings. Part of me felt horrible and guilty, the other part of me felt that he had driven me to it and he deserved what he got.

THERAPIST: I see. So you felt somewhat justified, but you also felt guilt.

FATHER: Yeah.

THERAPIST: I think hitting is something parents do when all else fails. I also don't think it works in the long run.

FATHER: It got his attention.

THERAPIST: Yeah, it gets their attention, but it doesn't keep their attention for very long. My prediction is that without any other interventions eventually he'll start being angry and provocative again.

FATHER: You're probably right.

THERAPIST: You want to use disciplinary techniques that have the potential to make long-term change.

FATHER: Well, yeah, unless it's too late.

THERAPIST: Well, I haven't met him yet but twelve is awfully young. I would be surprised if it was too late.

FATHER: What do you think we should do?

THERAPIST: Well, so far the things I notice are that you are using negative discipline, taking things away and punishing, rather than positive discipline such as rewarding him for behaviors you like.

MOTHER: Well, not too many of those lately.

THERAPIST: I know how that goes, sometimes you have to work hard to catch kids doing something that's good and to reward them for it. Can you think of a behavior you could reward?

FATHER: Well, the only thing I can think of is if he talks to us without screaming. Oh, and maybe if he came home when he was supposed to.

THERAPIST: Okay, so you came up with two things that might merit rewards. That's a good start. The other thing I've noticed is that it seems you've stopped communicating with him. You, Mr. S., are spending less "fun time" with him, and you, Mrs. S., don't seem to be spending as much time with him either, especially since you now have a job.

FATHER: Yeah.

THERAPIST: And one more thing. It seems like he maybe didn't adapt too well to his change in environment and maybe he's angry at not having a lot of control. When we adults make decisions like moving, kids often feel like they are being overlooked or that we don't care what they think or feel. Because of that, and because he's not responding well to limits, I would spend some time giving him a chance to negotiate with you, about curfews for example. He may be feeling like he's not being seen or heard very well, which may make him feel like he has to up the ante and yell and scream.

MOTHER: That's possible.

THERAPIST: How often have either of you used physical punishment?

FATHER: The last time I hit him he was seven years old and he started a fire in my office.

THERAPIST: Oh, oh. Did he learn his lesson?

FATHER: He seemed to. In a way, I think I might have contributed to that because I had taught him to make a fire when we were camping.

THERAPIST: How about you, Mrs. S.?

MOTHER: I've never hurt him and I never would. My parents hit me when I was a kid and I've always been scared of even raising my voice to him.

THERAPIST: How did you react the other day when Mr. S. punched Jasper?

MOTHER: That was very hard for me. I told him [Mr. S.] that.

THERAPIST: Okay, so it sounds like both of you would like to figure out other ways to discipline Jasper, and that's what we'll get on right away. In the meantime, I'd like you to think about the fact that Jasper may be acting out to get more of your attention, and I'd like you to plot a way to show him that you're interested. Then when I meet with you next time maybe we can see how to begin. I'd like to see Jasper on Thursday, and then we'll all meet together next week and start figuring out what will work. I'm sure if you're not happy with Jasper, he's probably not too happy either, so we'll try to get you guys communicating more clearly and get some rewarding exchanges going on. Right now all you can think of is how difficult he's been lately, but it sounds like you all were a lot happier when he was younger, and before you moved. You've got a history of good relations, that always helps.

FATHER: I wish I felt so optimistic.

THERAPIST: Well, I feel optimistic because of what you've told me, and the fact that part of you, maybe even most of you, would rather not hit your kid. Sounds like your wife doesn't like that either.

In this case, I found a way to have the parents describe the problem behaviors as well as prior efforts to ameliorate their concerns. I pointed out that their disciplinary techniques were ineffectual and produced only short-term results. I offered general guidelines about positive rather than negative strategies, and elicited positive memories about their interactions with their child. Both parents had some hesitancy about the effectiveness of physical punishment and seemed agreeable to my directives.

The father made an effort to spend time alone with Jasper; he became discouraged easily, however. Jasper was adept at exhibiting provocative behavior when he was alone with his father. Jasper's style of shutting down when his feelings were hurt did not serve him well, since it was his moodiness and lack of communication that most disturbed his father. There were two successful interventions for the family. For the first, I instructed the parents to bring out family pictures from their previous home and make sure that Jasper could overhear them talking about how much they missed their old home and town and how difficult the moved had been. They put on a slide show in the family living room and Jasper joined in, happy to see pictures of his old friends, as well as pictures of family activities.

The second intervention involved the parents' writing a joint letter to Jasper about how much they missed him, missed talking with him, doing things with him, sharing happy and sad times together, and so on. In the letter, the parents made no demands of Jasper; instead, they made a commitment to changing their own behavior and vowed to be more patient and more physically and emotionally available. In this letter, the parents invited Jasper to participate with them more, but assumed responsibility for making changes. Jasper responded well to the letter, letting his guard down from time to time, and apparently appreciating his parent's efforts.

Jasper was not physically abused again. He continued to object to curfews, and sometimes would test his parents' limits by coming home past the designated time. The parents imposed consequences for his behavior, removing privileges in a reasonable way, but their primary disciplinary approach became to reward Jasper for desired behaviors, to disengage from verbal sparring, and to accept Jasper's moodiness as part of adolescent transition. Interestingly, once Jasper's behavior became less outrageous, Jasper's mother became more outspoken about her own needs for her husband's time, and a period of marital therapy ensued.

Alternatives to Sexual Abuse

Familial child sexual abuse, whether between parents and children or between children, or extended family members, also emerges within the context of family dysfunction. In most incest cases, sex becomes a mechanism by which to exert power or control, to get intimacy needs met, or to resolve any of a number of emotional problems that cause a blurring of boundaries and inappropriate behavior.

The most frequent parental motivation to sexually abuse appears to be a compensatory need for power and control stemming from multiple factors, which often include a history of unresolved trauma, lack of maturity, and feelings of inadequacy or helplessness. The obvious imbalance of power between parents and dependent children creates an opportunity for such abuse of power.

To believe that power and control issues are exclusive motivators to sexual abuse is short-sighted, however, because it overlooks other possible motivators that may propel the behavior. I believe the first step in providing alternatives to sexual abuse is to determine the idiosyncratic nature of the problem. To do so, I usually make efforts to ascertain what precedes, occurs, and follows each episode of sexual abuse, recognizing that what motivates behavior may be different from what sustains the problem.

It may be possible, for example, that an individual rationalizes that he is educating his child about sexuality, and this rationalization precipitates the behavior, but the behavior is maintained by pleasurable physical sensations and by ego gratification from being in a position of control and power. Interventions address the cognitive error regarding the need to "educate" through demonstration, as well as breaking arousal patterns to children and finding appropriate ways to negotiate the desire to feel in control and powerful. These three separate dimensions require concurrent attention and specialized treatment services. In addition, because physical and sexual abuse of children is dangerous behavior, risk factors must be assessed and accountability must be well established. It is not sufficient to provide treatment focused on teaching alternative behaviors if an assessment has established an individual's impulsivity or other risk situation such as the use of drugs. Children who are in imminent danger of physical or sexual abuse or neglect must be in safe environments prior to treatment that focuses on teaching alternative behaviors.

Although some professionals believe that once parents commit sexual abuse they forfeit all parental rights, including the right to physically nurture their children in the future, I take a less extreme but cautious approach, due to my underlying belief that children need appropriate physical attention, nurturing, and modeling from both parents in order to maximize development, learn about gender roles, and achieve clarity on the need to distinguish love from exploitation or violence. The reintroduction of appropriate physical touch and nurturing can only be accomplished if the person who abuses acknowledges that sexual abuse is inappropriate and harmful to children, assumes full responsibility for initiating and controlling the behavior, and understands the nature of deviant arousal patterns, cognitive distortions, and relapse prevention strategies. In other words, some individuals who abuse can be rehabilitated and resume an effective parental role. However, a professional who specializes in working with individuals who abuse must feel confident that sufficient change has occurred before allowing the child to be reunited with the parent or encouraging safe and appropriate touching.

Once the individual who abuses understands the motivators for deviant arousal or behavior, alternative behaviors are identified and practiced. For example, if helplessness and hopelessness precede an individual's need to exert control over a child, the individual must learn what to do instead of approaching children. If the individual wants physical affection, he must learn how to get his needs met by adults. Learning to adopt alternative behaviors sounds deceptively easy, and yet due to the compelling nature of deviant arousal patterns and compulsive behaviors, the work of altering sexually abusive behaviors is arduous; prognosis tends to be guarded at best. At the same time, among individuals who offend, incestuous parents often motivate their behavioral changes by sincere affection for their children and a desire to keep their families intact.

In physical and sexual abuse, as well as in neglect cases, children are in danger. Clinicians must first safeguard the child's physical security, and then work on prevention strategies with parents who abuse so the threat of abuse will subside. Prevention work includes cognitive-behavioral strategies that identify the thinking errors and emotional states that precede and follow the abusive incidents. More often than not, clinicians must first rely on external accountability, encouraging the subsequent reliance on internal controls.

There is continued discussion in the professional community about whether to think about and approach incestuous fathers as if they were pedophiles. In my opinion, parents who sexually abuse their children are definitely pedophiles (that is, sexually aroused by children) and therefore must receive treatment specific to this condition. Distinguishing incestuous fathers from other pedophiles and providing differential treatment, particularly treatment that focuses on family dynamics and ignores deviant arousal patterns, is perilous.

Incestuous parents use varied justifications for the crimes they commit. Regardless of the fact that they often feel proprietary rights over their children, and often cite precipitators such as their spouse's unavailability, a desire to educate or prepare children, or a way to show children that they are loved or special, issues of narcissistic gratification of power, control, and sexuality inevitably enter the picture. I have found that in spite of the fact that incestuous parents justify or rationalize their initial motivations to have sexual contact with their children, arousal patterns to children are established and reinforced and can and often do generalize to other children. Therefore, parents who sexually abuse their children must engage in specialized treatment programs in which clinicians have comprehensive knowledge about sex offender treatment issues such as interrupting inappropriate arousal patterns, aversive and relapse prevention techniques, and the necessity of using legal and psychopharmacological resources. If you are not trained or qualified to provide these specialized services, it is best to find someone who is. If you are qualified, you must weigh the advantages and disadvantages of providing clinical services to all family members, including the person who abuses. For example, sometimes after you make the required report to child protective services, the person who abuses may find it impossible to view you as a helper, and may instead view you as an enemy. If this reaction cannot be subdued, you may not be the best therapist to provide treatment to this person. In addition, I have had occasions in which the parents decide to separate immediately after sexual abuse is discovered, and I become the primary therapist for the nonabusive parent and the children since the abusive parent becomes estranged from the family.

Lastly, there have been times when I have opted not to see a person who abuses due to countertransference responses that interfere with my ability to be helpful to that person. Over the years I have recognized that I cannot work with individuals who abuse infants or developmentally disabled children. I have also chosen not to work with sadistic offenders whose primary motivation to abuse seems to be the pleasure they find in inflicting pain on vulnerable children.

Alternatives to Neglect

Parents who neglect are unable or unwilling to provide basic and safe caretaking to their children. They are often overwhelmed by the demands of daily life and may withdraw physically and emotionally. Young children are particularly vulnerable in these situations since they are totally dependent on adults for their existence.

Parents who neglect need to be stimulated to attend to their children; often they need basic education about how to care for children, and may also be incapacitated by some external variable such as drug or alcohol use. Some neglectful parents are underfunctioning and infantilized and find it difficult to take care of themselves, let alone a young child. On occasion, parents' willingness to provide empathic care is hindered by their own neglectful histories or by developmental or cognitive delays that interfere with empathy (other-directedness) or motivation (relationships are perceived with skepticism and defensiveness).

Since the mid eighties, Homebuilder programs have emerged throughout the United States. These programs hold particular promise for neglecting families. They make use of trained volunteers who literally "move in" to prevent the child's institutionalization. The goal is to provide the parent with concrete in-home support and modeling of appropriate caretaking behaviors. Homebuilders teach parents how to clothe and feed their children, how to maintain a feeding and sleeping schedule, how to play with their offspring, and how to manage household responsibilities. Rather than providing parents with sophisticated abstract parenting principles, Homebuilders demonstrate appropriate and safe interactions in the hope that parents may imitate them and find their own accomplishments rewarding enough to motivate their future efforts. (To locate Homebuilders programs, contact your local child abuse prevention council, or inquire with child protective services workers.)

Neglecting parents need to be directed to attend to their children. They must be encouraged to take note of their children's physical traits, personality characteristics, and strengths and vulnerabilities. Often, learning new caretaking behaviors may allow parents to make clear distinctions about what was given to them and what is now available to their children.

Neglecting parents also need help to identify or express their emotions about their children to their children. For example, a parent may need to observe positive physical affection between the worker and the child in order to mimic the desired behaviors.

Alternatives to Emotional Abuse

Parents emotionally abuse their children in a variety of ways. Verbal abuse is one of the most frequent types. Verbal abuse includes berating, humiliating, browbeating, or attacking through tone, posture, and language. Often, the patterns of verbal abuse are so pervasive that the child receives primarily negative feedback that interferes with the development of positive self-regard or ego strength. In addition, children who are constantly criticized tend to internalize negative thoughts and emotions regarding their person, behavior, or accomplishments. These children may become withdrawn, depressed, and cautious, and may develop and utilize a range of psychological defenses to cope with daily barrages.

Parents need help to stop the persistence of negative comments. I ask parents to initially write down such comments rather than say them, and eventually to discard the piece of paper. I ask them to talk to themselves in the mirror so they might get a perspective on what it feels like to be on the receiving end. I ask them to take each negative word they use and define it (for example, one parent found humor in the fact that "horse's ass" actually meant the rear end of a horse and really had very little meaning). I may also ask parents to come up with less inflammatory words (for example, instead of calling a child "obstinate," the parent might call him or her "opinionated;" a child who is "screwy" might be called "unique" or "creative").

Whenever I'm working with emotionally abusive parents and their children, I model behaviors only after I have asked the parent to pay attention to what I am doing, and after I have told the parent that my behavior may or may not work, or may or may not work as easily for them. The parent must watch, repeat, rehearse, and experiment with parenting behaviors, since there is no guarantee that children will always respond well to new strategies.

If parents verbally abuse their children in my presence I stop them and ask them to use different language. Likewise, if parents hit their children in front of me, or sexualize their physical contact, I have no qualms in stopping them and demanding alternative behaviors.

Helping Parents to Depersonalize Children's Behavior

Parents who lash out at their children usually feel strong negative emotions, and their feelings have been hurt. A parent who is preoccupied by work pressures and trying to get a needed good night's sleep may perceive a child's waking up at night as a personal affront. The parent may in the heat of the moment feel, "This child is trying to get back at me." Instead of recognizing this behavior as typical of children, the parent personalizes that the child is out to get her. The parent is making an attribution to the child, which probably does not exist, and in doing so the parent allows herself to initiate an adversarial relationship. (I will discuss attributions later in this chapter.)

When parents personalize their children's behavior, I instruct them about child development and normalize the children's behavior in the context of developmental transitions. A parent who states that a child who is lying is "trying to make me look bad in front of my friends" may find it useful to know that children experiment with lying during a particular age, and that it is actually the most creative, resourceful, or bright children who behave in this way. Parents have sometimes found it useful to know that children will test out new behaviors (even if they are disruptive or provocative) with the people who love them most. It might be helpful for parents to learn that, contrary to their belief that a child who sasses back is disrespectful, sassing back is a behavior that children will often test out with a trusted parent.

In addition, I often take specific behaviors that parents find distressing and spend considerable time helping them explore other possible explanations for the behavior. "His breaking the toy you gave him may be his way of rejecting you, but I think it probably has something to do with something else. Any ideas what other explanations there might be?" This is often tedious work, and parents may not be able to come up with other explanations, in which case I might introduce a fictitious situation to make the point. "You know, I worked with another mom who used to feel that way. She was very surprised to find out that her child's breaking toys had something to do with his interest in molding, building, and dismantling, so she got him both Legos and clay to play with, and both mom and kid were pretty content after that."

Helping Parents Decode Children's Behavior

Another related issue addressed during treatment is parental ability to decode children's behavior and find concealed communications inherent in nonverbal behaviors. For example, when toddlers reach out their arms to their parents with a smile on their face, it is easy to understand that they want to be held. Likewise, as they grow, they are capable of playing a type of charades for their parents, often trying parental patience. I encourage parents to ask themselves frequently, "What could he be trying to say to me by what he's doing right now?"

A divorced Caucasian mother was irritated each time her six-year-old daughter commented that she wanted to be with her father or that her father had done or said something better than the mother. In response, the mother would scream, "If you love him so much, I can fix it so you can go live with him, you know, if he'll have you." Statements like this injured the child, who became less and less secure about her mother's love.

I asked the mother what she thought the child was trying to communicate when she talked about her father. The mother immediately responded, "That she wants to be with him."

"Which means what?" I said.

"That she doesn't want to be with me. No matter what I do, it's not good enough. It's not what she wants."

I then asked the mother how these thoughts made her feel, and she cried profusely about her feelings of worthlessness, fueled by her perception that she was a great disappointment to her daughter. It was easy to understand why she lashed out at her child, defending against her own painful feelings.

After she cried for a while and made her feelings known, I supported her by reminding her of all she had accomplished since her separation. She recognized that she had in fact mobilized herself to take proper care of herself and her child, and had made significant strides toward a safer, happier life.

I then shared with her that I thought she was too limited in the way she viewed her daughter's behavior:

THERAPIST: What I've noticed is that you are thinking about Debbie's complaining in only one way.

MOTHER: What do you mean?

THERAPIST: When you hear her mention her father, you think she's trying to tell you that she wants to be with him.

MOTHER: Yeah, mostly, or that he's better.

THERAPIST: That she prefers him.

MOTHER: Yeah.

THERAPIST: And when you think that, you start feeling bad about yourself, as a parent, and as a person.

MOTHER: I get mad.

THERAPIST: Right. You end up screaming at her, screaming mean things, because you don't want to feel hurt by the things you think she's saying.

MOTHER: I guess so.

THERAPIST: So my suggestion is that you let yourself think about Debbie's complaining in some other ways.

MOTHER: Like what?

THERAPIST: Well, I've got one idea, but there are probably others, too. My idea is that she's trying to make sure that you won't leave her, too.

MOTHER: What?

THERAPIST: Maybe, it's just one idea, when Debbie talks about her dad, she might be wanting reassurance that you aren't going to go away like her daddy did.

MOTHER: She should know better than that.

THERAPIST: Well, sometimes grown-up decisions and behaviors are difficult for kids to understand. She's only little.

MOTHER: I know. That's why I feel so bad when I scream those things at her.

THERAPIST: Yeah. The fact that you feel bad is your clue that you've probably hurt her feelings as well.

MOTHER: So, what should I say when she talks about her dad?

THERAPIST: Well, let's think about that together.

MOTHER: [Pause] I guess I could tell her that I'm here for her.

THERAPIST: Yeah, that's good. [Pause] Have you ever missed somebody?

MOTHER: Sure. I even miss him sometimes.

THERAPIST: Your ex?

MOTHER: Amazingly enough.

THERAPIST: I think that comes with any separation. You were together for ten years.

MOTHER: I guess.

THERAPIST: So maybe you can share with Debbie that you miss him.

MOTHER: But then she might think he's coming back. I hated that at first, how she couldn't understand he wasn't coming back.

THERAPIST: Well, maybe you can tell her you miss him and then make sure she knows that he isn't coming back.

MOTHER: Can I ask you something?

THERAPIST: Sure.

MOTHER: Why is it so hard for me to talk to her in a nice way?

THERAPIST: I'm not really sure about that. What's your guess?

MOTHER: I'm just not sure. I don't mean to be like I am with her. Sometimes I'm just so tied up in knots. I feel like . . . [wiping her tears] like I've ruined her life. I feel so guilty that she has to grow up without a father.

THERAPIST: I understand. We all want what's best for our children.

MOTHER: Well, that's just it. We really are better off without him, but I don't know, I still feel sad for her.

THERAPIST: Especially because you know what it's like to grow up without a dad.

MOTHER: Yeah. It was really hard. And my mom was so down all the time. Everything changed after he died.

THERAPIST: So, what you went through was really tough. And that can't be changed. But what can be changed is what you now create for Debbie.

MOTHER: It's an uphill climb.

THERAPIST: Yeap. No getting around that. The kind of changes you're making are tough. The good news is that there's lots of time to learn and try new things out with Debbie. I know how much you love her.

MOTHER: She's the world to me. I just wish I could show her how I feel.

THERAPIST: It's not always easy to show our feelings. But when there's a will, there's a way. And this might feel like hard work at first; eventually, you might build new habits you actually like.

As you can see, I tried to help this mother decode her child's behavior in a different way. She perceived Debbie's talking about her father as a rejection, which propelled her to say hurtful things to the child, mostly to keep herself from feeling guilt and pain. I suggested that there were many ways to decode Debbie's behavior and invited her to consider those possibilities. Eventually, the mother derived positive self-regard from decoding Debbie's behavior. Debbie liked her mother's attention and their positive interactions increased.

Teaching Parents How to Teach, Guide, and Discipline

All children require discipline, structure, and limits. Providing these ensures that children will develop a sense of safety and security, consistency, internal controls, and social skills, which prepare them for their interactions with others and their environment.

Over the years, professionals have introduced the concept of permissiveness, which has baffled parents and created uncertainty about appropriate parental responses. In addition, the words "discipline" and "corporal punishment" have become synonymous, creating perhaps one of the worst misunderstandings regarding childrearing.

Discipline is a must; corporal punishment is not! Numerous disciplinary techniques that do not depend on corporal punishment have been developed over the years. I try to teach parents positive parenting techniques that are respectful, cognizant of developmental stages and tasks, practical, individualized, and well rehearsed. I encourage parents to anticipate scenarios in which their children may need to be disciplined. During calm states, I direct parents to role play their responses, followed by actual practice through rehearsal at first with the therapist and later with their kids.

Many parents need to attend to two areas prior to learning positive parenting: impulse control, and avoiding out-of-control discipline. I instruct parents that impulsivity simply means thinking and acting at the same time. I then show them the drawing in Figure 3.1, which I initially used with children and later discovered to be equally instructional with adults.

As the figure illustrates, thoughts and actions are quite separate but joined by a platform. The idea is that when one has a thought, it is important to consider the consequences of doing what one has thought. The person is instructed to take one step at a time, considering a variety of consequences to taking action. On the platform is a superhero. I teach children that what makes this person a superhero is that he is able to make choices that have been carefully

FIGURE 3.1. Before Acting on Impulse, Consequences Must Be Evaluated and Clear Choices Made.

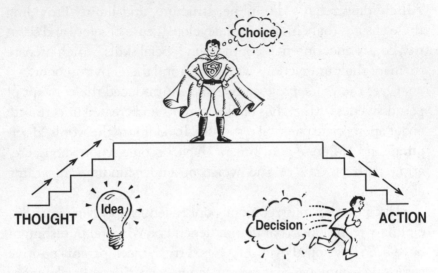

thought out. On top of the platform there is a better view, and once a decision is made, the person descends the stairway and engages in the activity.

I also give parents the concept of in-control and out-of-control discipline, and I encourage them to discipline their children only when they are feeling calm, clear-thinking, and considerate.

I often teach parents what to do to avoid out-of-control behavior when they feel they might become explosive. These steps are defined on a case by case basis, but may include putting the child in a safe place and removing oneself to another room; calling someone who can talk with them over the phone, including a crisis line; using available services, such as child care or respite care; asking for help from an already-established list of resource people, or seeking professional help from a crisis hotline, drop-in group, and so forth.

Parents who are volatile and prone to violent outbursts will need added attention. They may need to take specific actions, such as attending a violence abatement course, seeking professional help, or joining a self-help group specifically focused on developing channels for safe expression of anger. Parents' ability to control their violent behaviors must be carefully assessed when young children are living in the home. In addition, it is counterindicated to teach parenting skills that require empathy and impulse control to parents who do not possess those skills.

Henry Kempe (who coined the phrase "battered child syndrome") once made a statement in a lecture that has stuck with me throughout the years: "Teaching abusive parents Parent Effectiveness Training is like teaching people algebra who have not had basic math." It is important that we make careful and realistic choices about the disciplinary techniques we teach our clients.

Teaching Parents to Increase Rewarding Interactions with Their Children

As I discussed in Chapter Two, I evaluate the type and level of interactions between family members. With abusive or neglectful parents it's not unusual to find too many negative, inappropriate, or neutral interactions, with a paucity of positive ones.

If the level of negative or neutral interactions between parents and their children is high, parental motivation to spend time with their children will be low. This stands to reason. If parents have unrewarding, unsatisfactory, conflictual, and stressful interactions with their children, it would be expecting miracles for them to want to interact.

I encourage parents to think about and describe in great detail past interactions that were rewarding, positive, and loving. I have parents create mental images that can be retrieved quickly, and I encourage them to spend time remembering those specific events. I then ask parents to think about how to structure an interaction that has high potential for a rewarding consequence, and I help them identify a realistic plan for initiating possible pleasant contact.

When parents and children are truly battling and trust has been broken, the planning and implementing of potentially rewarding times can be difficult and challenging. One parent with whom I worked had such negative feelings toward her child that she confided being consumed with guilt and shame about disliking her daughter. She could not think of a single interaction that might be positive, so we first attempted a neutral one. Her idea was that she and her daughter could go to see a movie together since the mother liked almost all movies and viewed going to the movies as a high relaxation, low-stress activity. We talked about all the ways that this activity could become problematic, and once the mother acknowledged that buying candy could be a source of conflict, she decided to allow her daughter to eat anything she wanted. The daughter was excited to get spending money and defiantly said, "I'm gonna buy a lot of crap. It's my money." Mom said, "Whatever you want is okay, I'll meet you inside." Mom was surprised to find that her daughter made reasonable choices regarding junk food, and offered to share a popcorn bucket with her.

The experiment was successful because the preparation had been comprehensive, and the mother had been able to visualize conflict every step of the way and role play her responses.

Reducing Stress

Abusive parents rarely wake up in the morning plotting ways to hurt their children. In my experience, abusive parents more often than not love their children and are trying (as best they can) to be good parents.

Although no single variable causes abuse, stress has been found to be a significant contributor to violent behavior. Stress can have a cumulative effect that reinforces emotional conflict or feelings of helplessness. Probably no other variable elicits violence as much as helplessness, in fact, I often view violence and helplessness as opposite sides of the same coin.

Stress is felt differently by different people. Some individuals feel stress in their sore, aching, or ill bodies; others become listless and withdrawn, and choose to isolate themselves, feeling despondent and disenfranchised from humanity. Still others become agitated, irritable, and high-strung. The reactions vary as much as the remedies.

I discuss the issue of stress along physical, emotional, behavioral, and spiritual lines. I ask individuals to define stress and to talk about how they learned to cope with stress. I also inquire about people they know who are either devastated or untouched by the stress in their lives. In doing so, I normalize stress as a condition we all endure and must address in order to stay physically, psychologically, and spiritually healthy.

Luckily, there is no scarcity of books, pamphlets, videos, and audiotapes on stress reduction, stress inoculation, and specific techniques for reducing stress. I try to identify the manner in which the individual might best learn, and develop a program for addressing this important contributor to abuse and neglect.

Often, stress is caused by economic and environmental conditions such as unemployment, unavailable housing, crime-infested neighborhoods, and other realities. Consequently I make concerted efforts to assist my clients in accessing, negotiating, and obtaining needed assistance. When I work with abusive parents, I frankly assess their ability to mobilize resources on their own behalf. I instruct them about procedures and resources, and on occasion I take the initiative to get certain changes to occur that relieve the immediate stress and allow for subsequent improved parental functioning.

Teaching Parents Nonpunitive Responses

Sometimes parents are unaware that their responses are harsh and punitive. It might be surprising to parents who are full of good intentions that they may be overreacting to their children's misbehaviors, expecting too much, or holding children to impossible standards.

Often, parents who expect too much of their children expect too much of themselves as well. They may also feel insecure about their parenting skills, and may be overcontrolling as a way of dealing with their feelings of inadequacy.

I sometimes videotape parent-child interactions in an effort to help parents recognize the harshness in their tone of voice or their words. Other times I may show videotapes that present parents and children interacting, and lead a discussion based on reactions to the tape. Amazingly, some parents are very sensitive and responsive to the lessons presented in the videotapes, and appear very empathic to the children in those tapes. (One videotape I use with frequency shows three different parents who disclose problems with physical and emotional abuse and shows them interacting with their children. This tape is called *Family Circle* (1981) and was originally shown on public television. The tape is available by contacting the producer, Hali Paul. See the references for more information.)

Teaching Parents About Intimacy and Appropriate Affection

Touching (and other bonding behaviors) is another issue that many parents struggle to resolve to their satisfaction. Over the years I have worked with parents who were afraid to touch their children for fear they would hurt them, and parents who touched their children in intrusive ways. In addition, some parents seem unable or unwilling to offer nurturing behaviors to their children after they reach certain developmental ages or stages.

I invite parents to tell me about touching in their past and current families—who the huggiest people are, if there are some family members who seem to be particularly fond of or avoidant of touching, and so forth. I also inquire as to their own level of comfort with physical touching and other nurturing behaviors. In my experience, parents who have difficulties with physical affection come from families in which touching or emotional connectedness or bonding was inadequate. Growing up in emotionally disconnected families can have long-term implications for adult functioning in this domain (Karen, 1994).

After inquiring about this topic, I ask parents to visualize and report how they would like to incorporate touching into their family lives, and if they have seen other families who can serve as models (even television families). I then ask parents for behavioral descriptions, and a list of desired behaviors is compiled. If parents are learning to touch and touching seems unfamiliar or anxiety-provoking, they will need to approach touching slowly, increasing behaviors as they experiment and process their reactions.

Teaching Parents About Boundaries

Lastly, an area that seems to have positive or negative repercussions for family relationships is the issue of boundaries, and in my work with abusive or neglectful families, boundary issues abound.

I have family sessions in which boundaries are discussed. I ask for definitions of the term from parents and older youngsters. When the definitions are reviewed, I emphasize accurate descriptions and then add my own, delineating boundaries as the invisible rules about how people behave in relationships and how close to or far away from each other people remain. I give children the example that even though their teachers are helpful and friendly, they would not want to go on a double date with their teacher and his or her girlfriend or boyfriend. Smaller children understand that their physicians may give them shots and medicine, but their physicians do not come over to their house and have dinner with their parents or visit their school and help them with homework.

Eventually we talk about parent-child relationships, and I explain that there are enmeshed (too close) and disengaged (too far away) boundaries, and that families have to decide what is too much closeness, what is not enough, and what is just right.

I also do an exercise with parents and children that is designed to help them see each other as individuals who have their own space, and as individuals who must ask how close they can come to another person's space. This technique was developed by my colleague Enid Sanders, and she calls it the "magic circle." I help family members make circles on the floor with adhesive tape, which they then step inside. The magic circle symbolizes each person's boundaries. Each person standing in his or her own circle then invites others to approach, stopping people at comfortable distances. Every family member takes turns stopping others from coming too close or encouraging others to come closer. An adaptation of this technique was suggested by an audience member in one of my workshops, and when I tried it, I loved it. The suggestion was to have everyone hold a hula hoop around their body to clearly set up distances between people that must be negotiated and respected. Both of these techniques allow the abstract concept of boundaries to be understood on a much more concrete level.

Cognitive Restructuring

Once abusive behaviors are addressed, underlying thoughts and feelings emerge. Most abusive parents discover that their behaviors are propelled by conscious or unconscious beliefs, attitudes, or perceptions. The next task in therapy becomes to delineate associations between undesirable behaviors and established cognitive distortions that may have been generated by lessons learned in childhood (Bedrosian and Bozicas, 1994).

Parental Attributions and Misperceptions

When I work with parents who abuse in any way, I have found that helping them communicate about the abuse helps me to comprehend disguised or hidden motivations, perceptions, or feelings that catapult into dangerous behaviors. When parents deny insight, or too quickly narrow their understanding to one possible cause, I find it useful to dig deeper. Also, when parents make statements like, "This is the only way I know," or "This is the way it always is," I pursue the origins of these apparently rigid statements. The following example illustrates how a parent's negative attribution (of sexual badness) to a child caused her to perceive the child as threatening and inappropriate, eliciting a violent response. In other words, once the mother felt attacked by her child, she attacked back to protect herself.

A Caucasian mother of two children held her youngest boy on her hip while she waited for her preschooler to collect his things to go home. The preschool teacher called child protective services when she saw the mother suddenly and violently throw her child to the ground, causing the child to suffer lacerations on his head that required stitches. Child protective services referred the mother to me after receiving calls from both the hospital physician and the preschool teacher. The child was held in the hospital overnight and returned to the custody of his father (who lived with the mother), who was perplexed but not completely surprised about his wife's behavior. The child protective services worker decided to leave the child in the home after receiving the father's reassurance that his wife had never been violent before, and after ascertaining the mother's willingness to enter therapy immediately.

During the first meeting I could not succeed in creating a comfortable situation for the mother; she was on edge, hesitant, fearful, and obviously in crisis. She offered very little information, stating repeatedly that "no one could understand" what she had been through. During the second session she relaxed enough to ask me some questions about what could precipitate violence in someone who did not have a history of violent behavior. I responded generically, offering her some information about precipitators of violence. Mainly, I confided to her that we would need to understand more about her thoughts and feelings.

The following exchange occurred during the last fifteen minutes of the session and set the context for the rest of therapy.

THERAPIST: Maybe what we can do is talk very specifically, in a kind of slow-motion manner, about what was going on right before you threw the baby down.

MOTHER: I guess . . . [sobbing] since it happened I haven't wanted to, you know, really think about it too much.

THERAPIST: That's understandable. This was a shock not only to those around you, but to you as well.

MOTHER: [Sobs] I'm not like that. That's not me. I've been so upset. You don't know. . . .

THERAPIST: Lucy, I've heard you say that lots of times, that I won't or others won't understand what's happened to you.

MOTHER: You won't, nobody will. Even I don't [*sobs*]. . . .

THERAPIST: I can see how confused and upset you are. Take your time.

MOTHER: What was the question?

THERAPIST: I wanted to talk about the day that you threw your baby on the ground.

MOTHER: Oh yeah, okay, okay. [*Blowing her nose*] I don't know exactly what you want to know.

THERAPIST: You picked your other child up at his school at about one P.M., is that right?

MOTHER: Yes, Monday, Wednesday, and Friday I pick him up at one P.M.

THERAPIST: How had your morning been?

MOTHER: Okay.

THERAPIST: What had you done?

MOTHER: Same old, same old. The baby had just gotten up from his morning nap and he was fine, then it was time to go.

THERAPIST: So nothing unusual happened that morning.

MOTHER: No, nothing special.

THERAPIST: How were you feeling?

MOTHER: Okay. Same as usual.

THERAPIST: Which is what?

MOTHER: What's what?

THERAPIST: How do you usually feel?

MOTHER: Oh, alright. I mean I don't even think about it anymore.

THERAPIST: Have you had happier times?

MOTHER: Yeah.

THERAPIST: When were you happier?

MOTHER: When I was younger.

THERAPIST: How old?

MOTHER: Early twenties. That was the best time for me.

THERAPIST: I see.

MOTHER: It's a long story.

THERAPIST: And we'll get into it sometime soon, but right now I'd like to go back to the day you threw your son.

MOTHER: I'm sorry. I feel so scatterbrained right now.

THERAPIST: No need to apologize. I know there's a lot going on for you right now. I'd like you to imagine yourself standing there at the school, waiting for your older boy to pick up his stuff so you could drive back home.

MOTHER: Yeah, I remember. I was standing right inside the front door, next to the kids' little cubbies where they keep their stuff.

THERAPIST: Okay. Now tell me what happens next.

MOTHER: I was watching Jimmy get his stuff out of his cubby and I was trying to keep the baby from jumping out of my arms.

THERAPIST: What do you mean? How were you holding him?

MOTHER: Just usual. On my hip, with my arm under his butt.

THERAPIST: And what was he doing?

MOTHER: He had his feet dug into my hip and he was bouncing.

THERAPIST: Bouncing how?

MOTHER: Bouncing up and down.

THERAPIST: And if you put words to that behavior, what would the child be saying to you?

MOTHER: I . . . [*sobbing and covering her eyes with her hands*] Oh, my God, I remember now, I remember. He was . . . humping . . . humping me.

THERAPIST: How do you mean?

MOTHER: Humping me . . . humping . . . being dirty with me.

THERAPIST: Do you mean sexual?

MOTHER: Yes, oh God, yes.

THERAPIST: How did the baby bouncing up and down get to feel sexual to you?

MOTHER: Because . . . [*uncontrollable sobbing*] his father, his father. . . .

THERAPIST: Tell me about his father.

MOTHER: His father . . . he was a pervert . . . a pervert.

THERAPIST: What do you mean?

MOTHER: He raped, raped me.

THERAPIST: Your younger son's father raped you?

MOTHER: Yes.

THERAPIST: Is he your current husband?

MOTHER: No, it was a stranger, not my husband.

THERAPIST: Does your husband know about the rape?

MOTHER: Oh God, no. He wouldn't stand it, couldn't stand knowing. I couldn't tell him. He'd be impossible.

THERAPIST: How so?

MOTHER: He's always harping on how I shouldn't go out alone. And this happened in a parking lot, after I went shopping.

THERAPIST: Were you able to get a medical exam?

MOTHER: No, I couldn't do that either. I just went home, took lots of showers, scrubbed myself raw, and just cried. I didn't sleep all night.

THERAPIST: I'm really sorry. That must have been horrible for you, and not having any support during that time must have felt terrible.

MOTHER: It did. [*Long pause*]

THERAPIST: How are you feeling now?

MOTHER: It feels funny to have finally told somebody about it.

THERAPIST: I'm glad you were able to do that. Keeping distressing things like this secret can really be difficult.

MOTHER: The worse part was when I got a positive pregnancy test.

THERAPIST: Did you do it yourself at home?

MOTHER: Yeah, one of those blue stick things.

THERAPIST: And what did you think when you were for sure pregnant?

MOTHER: I was scared to death. I didn't know what to do.

THERAPIST: You were sure it wasn't your husband's?

MOTHER: That was for certain. We hadn't been together that often. As a matter of fact, right after I found out and I decided I couldn't have an abortion, I felt I had to sleep with him so that he wouldn't think it was weird that I was pregnant.

THERAPIST: And how did he react to your pregnancy?

MOTHER: He didn't seem to care one way or another. I'm the one who takes care of them. He's hardly ever home, and he's, you know, like most guys I guess, just kind of on the outskirts.

THERAPIST: You feel he's not as involved as he could be.

MOTHER: No, except right now, because he has no choice.

THERAPIST: Oh, you mean because otherwise they might have removed your children from your care.

MOTHER: Yeah.

THERAPIST: So some things about what happened in the school that day are more clear now.

MOTHER: Maybe.

THERAPIST: Well, it seems that you threw the child to the ground to get him off you, because you felt he was being sexual with you.

MOTHER: I've never been able to really love him like my older child.

THERAPIST: How do you feel about him?

MOTHER: I'm a God-loving woman and I tried very hard to love him. I've always kept him fed and clean and taken good care of him.

THERAPIST: And how did you feel toward him?

MOTHER: Like he was my punishment, a reminder of something bad that happened that I kept secret because of my shame.

THERAPIST: And you've never been violent with him?

MOTHER: No, if anything, I've been very careful with him, I've avoided showing him any of my feelings. Mostly I let him play by himself. His brother spends lots of time with him, talking to him and such.

THERAPIST: Well, it seems like we have a lot of work in front of us.

MOTHER: What do you mean?

THERAPIST: Well, I think we need to talk some more about your feelings toward your child, and you may want to talk some more about the rape, and we generally need to make sure that the same response that happened when you threw the child won't happen out of the clear blue again. I'm certainly willing to help you sort all this out, help you decide how you feel and what you want to do.

MOTHER: You know, just one more thing since I'm spilling

my guts. I would have been very relieved if they had taken the baby somewhere for a while. I was excited when I heard that they might take him. Isn't that horrible?

THERAPIST: No, not horrible. I think it's honest. It sounds like you've had really confusing and difficult emotions about your son for a long time and I can understand how you might have wanted a break.

MOTHER: Yeah, a break from being reminded every day.

THERAPIST: What do you mean?

MOTHER: This child is the spitting image of his father.

THERAPIST: Really?

MOTHER: My two kids don't look anything alike.

THERAPIST: I see.

MOTHER: Sometimes strangers in the park ask if they're cousins or something.

THERAPIST: That must be hard for you to be reminded of something you've tried so hard to put behind you.

MOTHER: Yeah, good job I've done so far, huh?

I worked with this mother for nine months, and she made considerable progress. She talked about the rape and expressed pent-up emotions she had experienced for eighteen months. She eventually realized that she had not caused the rape, but rather had been in the wrong place at the wrong time. She recognized rape as an act of violence and acknowledged that she could not separate her child from his father in her own mind. After six months of therapy she told her husband about the rape and brought up the possibility of putting the baby up for adoption. At the same time, she broached the subject of separating from her husband, stating clearly that "the marriage died years ago." The parents decided to place the child for adoption after brief discussions about the father's interest in continuing to care for both children.

This was a tragic situation for all parties, particularly for the older child, who had been the primary caretaker for his younger brother. The mother got her older child into therapy to cope with the separation.

This mother exemplifies the process of attribution very accurately. She made attributions of sexual badness to her child and then responded to him as though he did in fact present a sexual threat. She was predisposed to see the child in this way because he was the product of a rape. Throwing the child to the ground was her way to protect herself from perceived sexual attack. The therapy allowed the mother to evaluate her life and take steps on her own behalf.

Therapy may also encourage parents to learn and use alternative behaviors that keep children safe. To make necessary changes, parents need to view their children's behavior realistically, decoding and depersonalizing their requests and behaviors.

Addressing Parental Misperceptions

Many parents misperceive their children's behavior. For example, a parent may view an infant's crying as the child's way "to bug me," or "to get back at me." I always try to ascertain parental perceptions because they often precipitate inappropriate parental responses. It is important to help parents broaden their perceptions so they are able and willing to consider a range of possibilities rather than using tunnel vision. When a parent views a normative behavior such as children wetting their diapers as a way that the children are trying to manipulate the parent, I ask them to consider other possibilities, such as the fact that diaper wetting is a normative bodily function that keeps the child healthy.

I also ask parents to talk to other parents to obtain divergent ideas and perspectives that might help broaden their own views. I find it useful to make definitive statements such as, "You know, being a good parent is a tough job that most of us didn't go to school to learn about, so we have to fall back on what we learned from our parents as children or whatever else we pick up from books or classes or friends. Sometimes we goof. We look at a particular thing and we think it means something that it doesn't mean. Like when you look at how dirty your child is and you think he's trying to make you look like a bad parent. What's really happening is that the child played in dirt and got dirty. That can happen to anyone. You're reading too much into it. Kids don't think in devious ways; they're too little to plot against their parents."

On occasion, destructive parental perceptions remain rigid and cannot be altered. One parent called her child "pus" and considered him damaged, ineffectual, and beyond repair. The child had no problematic behavior; he elicited his mother's hostility simply because he looked like his maternal grandfather, by whom she had been beaten, and this resemblance put the child at risk of her retaliation. She could find nothing positive about him. She had taken care of all his needs during his infancy, but when he took on what she viewed as traditional male characteristics, she rejected and humiliated him in order to keep herself feeling safe. This child represented a threat, and she felt she had to control him in every possible way in order to contain her own anxiety and expectation of being hurt.

This parent had many disturbances in her ability to see her child realistically and she eventually approached child protective services voluntarily for an out-of-home placement. The child thrived in foster care and remained there until he was eighteen. In this case, separating was the best alternative for both mother and child.

Another example that illustrates how clinicians must directly confront inappropriate misperceptions involved the father of a sexually abused ten-year-old. The child reluctantly disclosed the sexual abuse to her favorite teacher after hearing a presentation on "good/bad touching." The father vehemently denied the allegation and contacted a group for "falsely accused" fathers, who encouraged him to file a lawsuit against the school for exposing his child to inflammatory and unclear information that elicited his daughter's "false allegation." The lawsuit was dropped when the school produced the mother's signed consent form that allowed her child to participate in the educational program presented by a child abuse prevention program.

The district attorney who investigated the case and videotaped his interview with the child showed the videotape to the child's father, at which point the father plea bargained to a lesser charge in exchange for his participation in therapy. His sentence was commuted and he was placed on probation for one year with mandatory treatment. He also agreed to leave his home for a minimum of six months, after which time a case review would be held.

His participation in therapy was guarded, although after four months he came to the conclusion that he needed to discuss the abuse directly if he ever hoped to reconstitute his family. Eventually he felt it was in his best interests to cooperate fully with therapy that included individual, group, and family components. Fortunately for him, he was in a financial position to both support two households and purchase therapeutic services for himself and his family.

After the father was no longer in denial about undressing his daughter, fondling her, and masturbating to fantasies of her naked body, the following communication took place:

FATHER: I can't tell you I feel really bad about it. Mostly I don't think it hurt her. I mean, she didn't say no, and she didn't cry, and once she even told me it felt good.

THERAPIST: Okay, so let's take those ideas one by one. When you say you didn't hurt her, what do you mean?

FATHER: I didn't, you know, rape her, or hurt her in any way. I was really gentle.

THERAPIST: So you're talking about physical hurts.

FATHER: Huh? Yeah, I guess so.

THERAPIST: And is that the only kind of hurt?

FATHER: No, I know. You can also hurt someone emotionally.

THERAPIST: Right. And given that you're the parent and she's the child, I'm sure you can see how that might make you a pretty powerful person to her, and that she might be vulnerable to you and your wishes and thoughts and feelings.

FATHER: I know, I know [*irritated*].

THERAPIST: You say that as if you're tired of hearing it.

FATHER: Well, it's not really an original thought, you know? I know the status I have with her. She's a little kid, she loves me, she trusts me.

THERAPIST: Exactly. And that makes her vulnerable. It's not only that she's little and depends on you and looks up to you, it's also that you're one of the most important people in her life.

FATHER: [*Quietly*] And she to me.

THERAPIST: Okay. I know you love your daughter, but it's not okay to take advantage of the love she has for you.

FATHER: I know.

THERAPIST: Now, let's go back to some of the things you said earlier. She didn't say no, was that it?

FATHER: Well, yeah. I said to myself that as long as she didn't say no, then I wasn't really taking advantage of her.

THERAPIST: First, let me ask you if you think there might have been any way she said no without using words.

FATHER: You mean pushing me away?

THERAPIST: Well, you already said she didn't do that. I'm wondering, for example, how she held her body when you were touching her vagina.

FATHER: She just lay there.

THERAPIST: You mean she lay still?

FATHER: Uh huh.

THERAPIST: Describe her body to me. Did she open her legs, was she dressed, did she raise her skirt, how did it happen?

FATHER: Well, I did most of the . . . work . . . you know.

THERAPIST: Describe it to me step by step.

FATHER: Well, although I think it's a little weird to talk about this. . . .

THERAPIST: What do you mean, "weird?"

FATHER: You know, uncomfortable.

THERAPIST: Okay. Tell me about it anyway.

FATHER: It was in the night. I stayed up and watched the late shows, flipping around, trying to unwind from work.

THERAPIST: And where was your wife?

FATHER: Upstairs, asleep. She goes to bed at about nine every night. They both go to bed around that time.

THERAPIST: Okay, so you flip around the channels and you stay up until when, 12:30 or 1:00?

FATHER: About then.

THERAPIST: Go 'head.

FATHER: Then I'd go upstairs to bed, and usually I didn't plan to go into her room but sometimes when I passed her room the urge got too strong.

THERAPIST: And then what?

FATHER: I tried not to wake her. I just pulled her undies down and once they were off I spread her legs open. Then I rubbed her gently with my fingers.

THERAPIST: Did you put your fingers inside her?

FATHER: Sometimes.

THERAPIST: Did she wake up when you did that?

FATHER: Well, sometimes she woke up right away and she called out my name.

THERAPIST: How did she do that?

FATHER: She said, "Daddy."

THERAPIST: Do you think it was a greeting?

FATHER: Yeah, in a way, I don't really know. I know she knew I was there.

THERAPIST: And then what?

FATHER: Sometimes I licked her gently. That's when she said she liked it.

THERAPIST: What exactly did she say?

FATHER: That it tickled.

THERAPIST: And you took that to mean she liked it.

FATHER: Well, yeah. She said it tickled.

THERAPIST: Do you think it's possible that it tickled her but that she wasn't making a definitive statement that she liked what you were doing?

FATHER: I guess so.

THERAPIST: Did you ever put your penis inside her vagina?

FATHER: Oh God, no. I could tell, in all humility, that there was no way I could get my penis inside her. She was just way too small. My finger was almost too big. I would lick my finger so that my finger could go in more easily.

THERAPIST: Did you get an erection doing this?

FATHER: I got an erection walking into the room. There's just something about her little body, and her little bald vagina, there's something exciting about how small it is, and how big my finger and tongue feel.

THERAPIST: What did you do with your erection?

FATHER: I jacked off into a Kleenex. Sometimes I . . . never mind.

THERAPIST: What were you going to say?

FATHER: It sounds really sick now but if I couldn't get off I'd go wake my wife up and I'd come really quick, almost as soon as I pushed inside her.

THERAPIST: Back to your daughter. What did you do before you left her room?

FATHER: I pushed her legs back together, put her undies on, covered her up, kissed her goodnight, and went to bed.

THERAPIST: And how often was she awake?

FATHER: I think she was awake most of the time. I think she liked it.

THERAPIST: Why do you think that?

FATHER: Because she didn't push me away. If she had done that, or said no, I wouldn't have continued.

THERAPIST: What I was getting at earlier is that sometimes young children don't feel they can say no through words, but they do things like pretend to be asleep, pretend to be unaffected, pretend not to feel anything.

FATHER: I don't know about that. How would I know?

THERAPIST: Well, you've been thinking about some things meaning one thing but it's possible they could mean something else. For example, the fact that she said her vagina tickled when you licked her doesn't mean she likes it and wants more, and even if she has physiological responses at being touched in her genitals, it's not okay for her father to be touching her genitals. If anything, she should be allowed to develop a gradual interest in sexuality, not have it imposed on her because of your adult needs. And the fact that she wasn't able to say no doesn't mean that her body's stiffness wasn't her way of saying no, or her pretending to be asleep wasn't a way of showing her discomfort or pain.

FATHER: I don't know.

THERAPIST: You need to think about these things. Even if she didn't say no in words or actions, which I doubt. Tell me how she said yes.

FATHER: How she said yes?

THERAPIST: Yeah, you said you would have stopped if she said no. How did she say yes?

FATHER: She didn't really say yes.

THERAPIST: Are you sure?

FATHER: I guess so.

THERAPIST: You guess, or you're sure?

FATHER: I guess I'm sure.

THERAPIST: Okay, let's not play word games. This is stuff I really want you to get clear about.

FATHER: Okay, I'm sorry.

THERAPIST: Now, before we end our meeting today, and because you've been very forthcoming about details today, is there anything else about your daughter that somehow confused you or made you feel she was being sexy [*a word he had used to describe his daughter in the past*].

FATHER: The only other time was when she used to run around the house naked.

THERAPIST: What do you mean, "run around the house naked"?

FATHER: Well that's an exaggeration, but sometimes after she took a shower she walked by the bedroom without her clothes on.

THERAPIST: Is your bedroom on the way to her room?

FATHER: Yeah, she had to go by, but she could have put her towel on her body instead.

THERAPIST: Instead of where?

FATHER: Her hair.

THERAPIST: She has really long hair, doesn't she?

FATHER: Down to her waist.

THERAPIST: I can see how she might want to wrap it up in a towel, it probably takes a long time to dry. How was it that you could see her walk by?

FATHER: Well, I did sort of listen for her . . . kind of watch out for her to come out.

THERAPIST: So it doesn't sound like she was parading around hoping you would see her.

FATHER: No, but she wasn't hiding either.

THERAPIST: And when she took these walks. How often did they occur?

FATHER: Well, actually they didn't occur too often.

THERAPIST: Number of times?

FATHER: Probably twice.

THERAPIST: Recently, or over what span of time?

FATHER: In the last few years.

THERAPIST: I see. So this behavior was extremely infrequent.

FATHER: Oh yeah.

THERAPIST: And yet you thought of it as her being sexy with you.

FATHER: Well, both times her mother wasn't around.

THERAPIST: So you thought she wanted you to see her, that she was being sexual with you.

FATHER: Well, I used to think that. I'm not so sure I do now.

THERAPIST: What changed your mind?

FATHER: Well, just reading in that book that kids sometimes experiment with their bodies, showing or not showing it to their parents.

THERAPIST: In any case, just because a child is naked, that is not an invitation to be touched in a sexual way. Imagine if every scantily clothed child was sexually abused?

As you can see, this father had serious misperceptions or thinking errors that allowed him to rationalize his behavior and to view his daughter's responses as compliant, even cooperative. His perceptions of these events had to be challenged in order to break through his denial, to help him assume full responsibility for abusing his daughter, and to work on arousal patterns so he could learn how to control his inappropriate urges in the future.

This family did not find a way to reestablish trust and reunify. The child had severe emotional problems as a result of her father's abuse. The mother eventually remarried and the father had sporadic supervised contact with his daughter until she was older and felt comfortable visiting him voluntarily.

Challenging Parental Attitudes and Beliefs

It is important to identify the origins of parental attitudes and beliefs about caretaking. I usually ask specific questions about a number of caretaking functions (nutrition, sleeping, toilet training, discipline, developmental tasks, sexuality, and so forth), and if parents find it difficult to be specific, I ask them to read some vignettes and jot down their responses. Often, asking parents to comment on generic situations gives clinicians an accurate view of their morals, values, attitudes, and beliefs.

When belief systems contribute to their abusive behaviors (for example, the belief that it is important to hit kids or they do not learn), I ask parents to explain how the beliefs became established, and then I challenge them to review, revise, and adapt those beliefs based on new information.

When working with belief systems that emerge from cultural beliefs and practices, it is helpful to explore how such ideas become embedded in specific cultures. For example, a culture may have a history of women being oppressed physically and sexually, and individuals within the culture may have come to recognize these behaviors as expected or as the norm. That a cultural history includes oppression of women or children does not mean that individuals within cultures cannot make choices about how to lead their lives. As a personal example, in Latin American countries many married women acknowledge and tolerate infidelity since traditionally men have had mistresses and illegitimate children. These behaviors are accepted by both men and women and they are based on a climate in which women are financially dependent, do not believe in divorce, and shy away from independent living. Therefore, the belief systems are rarely challenged and the status quo continues. Being bicultural and having been exposed to different cultural practices, I was able as an adult to make decisions about how I conducted my personal relationships without imposed or forced choices.

The same challenge applies to religious beliefs that support abusive practices. I have had many encounters with parents who physically abuse their children and quote scriptures such as "spare the rod, spoil the child." It appears that certain religions believe that corporal punishment is absolutely necessary to educate children (which I do not believe), and parents who adhere to these religions and who abuse feel justified in using corporal punishment as a way to shape moral character in children. Unfortunately, there is a fine line between corporal punishment and child abuse, and some parents take corporal punishment to extremes that result in child injuries.

I sometimes encourage abusive parents to take their questions to religious leaders. This sometimes backfires, but often ministers, rabbis, priests, and others have the authority to discuss religious scriptures, and will differentiate between corporal punishment and violence.

Discussing Family-of-Origin Issues

Family-of-origin issues are at the root of many inappropriate parenting behaviors, as well as inaccurate ideas about children. Although the research on cross-generational transmission processes is inconclusive, clinical observations consistently reveal correlations between adult caretaking patterns that are abusive or neglect-ful and prior abuse/neglect histories. At the same time, specific inci-dents of abuse and neglect or a chronicity of abusive or neglectful patterns emerge or continue as a result of sociocultural factors that exacerbate or permit these behaviors.

The research indicates that many individuals who hurt children have histories of physical and sexual abuse. However, not everyone who was abused in childhood becomes an abusive adult; a host of mediating variables come into play.

In my experience, unresolved histories of childhood trauma often permeate adult caretaking. In these cases, treatment must focus on resolving childhood issues and teaching alternative care-taking behaviors. This is much easier said than done.

Histories of childhood abuse do not predict abusive parenting behaviors. Many survivors of childhood abuse choose not to have children, or because of their difficult childhoods, they make con-certed efforts to prepare themselves for parenting by taking educa-tional classes, spending time with nieces or nephews, going to therapy to discuss fears and concerns, or becoming child-care providers. Although histories of childhood abuse may or may not result in repetition of abusive or neglectful behaviors, many parents who abuse appear to be influenced by their early lessons about inti-macy, physical attention, nurturing, displays of emotion, and so forth. It also appears that unresolved conflicts in identity, as well as impaired senses of safety or security, self-esteem, and self-reliance may impel specific interactional difficulties.

The Cultural Context and Historical Legacies

The functioning of individuals within society is shaped in part by precedents set in social history. When we review the history of chil-dren, as far back as one looks children have been treated bleakly. In his valuable review of the history of child abuse and infanticide, Radbill (1974, p. 6) documents that the Patria Postestas (an ancient Roman law) endowed the father with the privilege to "sell, abandon, offer in sacrifice, devour, kill, or otherwise dispose of his offspring." The practice of infanticide, condoned for many centuries, anthropologically refers to "the killing of a newborn with the consent of parent, family, or community" (Radbill, 1974, p. 6).

Unfortunately, adults have never lacked abusive or exploitive ways to misuse and maltreat children. It has taken centuries to organize and implement a child welfare system whose primary task it is to protect not just wayward and abandoned children, but children who need protection from their biological parents (once considered to have absolute rights regarding their children).

These legacies persist even today. The discussion about parental versus children's rights continues unabated, and in the current climate of "false memories" and "false allegations" the public is often swayed to view children as malicious accusers or liars. Individual incidents of abuse and neglect occur within this social context, which alternately and sporadically focuses on or avoids the plight of children across the world. Every now and then, horrific tales serve as chilling reminders of the potential of parents to commit cruel and unusual harm to their offspring.

As I was preparing this manuscript during the winter of 1994, the case of Susan Smith of South Carolina dominated the print and visual media. Ms. Smith, a twenty-three-year-old separated mother of two (Michael, three, and Alexander, fourteen months) tearfully pleaded for her young children's safe return after she claimed that an African American male had forced her out of her car and absconded with her children. After nearly ten days of a nationwide search for the children, the FBI and sheriff's office announced that the mother had confessed to the killing of her young children and that she would be charged with two counts of premeditated murder.

I happened to be conducting a training in South Carolina during the initial search for the children and talked with many local people about this tragedy. I also talked with many individuals after the murder charges were brought against the mother, and was among those who were shocked and distressed over the news. At the same time, it was sobering to hear Ann Cohn Donnelly, Director of the National Center for the Prevention of Child Abuse, tell a morning television audience that "three children are murdered each day." Although this case had captured the attention of the country, Ms. Cohn Donnelly was quick to point out that it was not an isolated instance. Indeed, she stated, two to three thousand children die from abuse or neglect each year.

In 1993, another highly visible case involved Joey Buttafuco, a married man in his mid thirties, and Amy Fisher, an adolescent with whom he had an alleged romantic affair. Amy Fisher was sentenced to prison for shooting Mrs. Buttafuco in the face with a pistol, claiming that she did it at Mr. Buttafuco's insistence. Three two-hour movies were devoted to the Amy Fisher story, often touted as a "Lolita." The fascination with childhood sexuality is also evident in print ads. A current top model whose face has appeared on the most popular magazines is sixteen years old, and she has been modelling successfully since she was thirteen. An extreme example of the marketability of children's sexuality is the fact that the United States has the second largest child pornography market, lagging behind only Denmark in production and exportation.

Although many would argue that positive changes have occurred in both women's and children's status in this country, it would be necessary to add that women and children of color may not reap the benefits of these changes. Current social conditions have created an array of pressing problems: random violence in the streets, carjacking, drug abuse, violent gang activities, rapes, kidnapping, child pornography, and prostitution. Consequently, public feelings of helplessness and fear now permeate our society.

We have also seen an increase in homeless individuals and families in our country, forcing communities to address issues of poverty, unemployment, drug abuse, and lack of resources for mentally ill or physically or developmentally delayed individuals. These are serious and real social ills, and their very presence may indicate a flawed and poorly prioritized government system that does not allocate its resources well enough to protect children in all walks of life. In this context, neglectful parents must be assessed carefully to ascertain whether they are unwilling or unable to provide basic caretaking to children rather than incapacitated by poverty, lack of resources, and lack of access to helping agencies. At the same time, the practice of encouraging families to survive through welfare support must be adapted to provide assistance such as education and training to families and children.

In a country rich in resources, it is hard to fathom that children would go hungry, die from lack of medical attention, or not be able to access housing or education. Yet these are some of the realities of family life for a large population of children. This is the context in which individual episodes of abuse and neglect occur. The specifics of a problem situation cannot be addressed without assessing and confronting the ample framework in which the problems emerge. When we attempt to address individual errors in thinking, we must concurrently deal with social messages that influence and reinforce individual belief systems.

This chapter advances numerous ideas that I have found useful in my work with abusive parents. First and foremost, I believe that a systemic approach is pivotal in understanding the complex dynamics in families in which abuse surfaces. Cognizance of how all family members both contribute to and are influenced by child abuse will allow for realistic and comprehensive interventions that do not unintentionally overlook any individuals in the family system. Furthermore, once clinicians understand the nature and extent of family members' contributions to creating or sustaining the problem behavior, the focus of treatment is on children's safety. Consequently, rigorous efforts converge on the abusive behavior. I believe that there are various dimensions to focusing on the symptom of abuse. Clinicians must provide alternative behaviors; they must address cognitive distortions, including misattributions, misperceptions and inappropriate belief systems; they must assess how historical factors, such as abuse in their own childhoods, influence current parental childrearing practices; they must evaluate how cultural and religious beliefs contribute to or reinforce inappropriate convictions and corresponding behaviors; they must help parents break isolation; and they must build internal and external resources. Therapy must often be nontraditional, including home visits or home-based programs (see for example, Berg, 1994), and they must provide clear alternative behaviors that parents can comprehend, practice, and incorporate. Lastly, therapy must be provided by clinicians who feel comfortable using their authority, providing directive interventions, and using crisis-intervention strategies, who have familiarity with community resources, and who can consider solution-focused approaches.

4

Beginning Treatment

Systemic treatment contemplates a broad range of interacting variables including family organization and structure; how symptoms are created and maintained; how each family member contributes to creating a climate in which a particular symptom appears and continues; how individual family members perceive and respond to specific problems; how they access and use internal and external resources; and how the family interacts with extended family, community, and their historical and current social and cultural environments. In child abuse cases, a systemic approach regards abuse as a manifestation of underlying dysfunctions and prioritizes children's safety and a restoration of appropriate and secure uses of power and control. Furthermore, systemic treatment empowers victimized individuals by setting firm limits on misuses of power, advocating for disempowered or injured individuals, and providing clear alternative responses to abuse behavior. Interventions proceed in an orderly fashion, addressing abusive behaviors first, followed by attention to underlying motivators.

The first phase of treatment therefore includes an assessment of high-risk behaviors and addresses abusive behavior, establishing external controls, and identifying cognitive distortions that contribute to or sustain problem behaviors. Clinical decisions are made about the feasibility of providing treatment to the family with the abusive person in the home. Treatment will have optimal impact when children are safe from ongoing abuse. Clinicians are encouraged to consult with investigators and make joint decisions regarding children's continuing safety.

In the second phase of treatment, persistent efforts are made to elicit the development of and reliance on internal controls. In addition, unresolved histories of childhood abuse, which often create obstacles to desired change, and other relevant issues are addressed and resolved.

The third phase of treatment is concerned with decisions regarding separation or reunification, and with prevention strategies for the future.

Using a Systemic Approach

There has been ongoing discussion among clinicians and researchers about the advisability of specific treatment modalities, strategies, and techniques in working with families who abuse. Systemic work has often been discarded in rather cavalier fashion by those who perceive the systemic approach to be counterindicated in families with abuse problems.

In particular, the most consistent argument posed against family therapy or systemic work is a simplistic and misinformed view of systemic therapy as restoring or fortifying a power base for abusive parents (especially sexual offenders) who are seen as having predominantly power-based behaviors. The argument presumes that family therapists are focused on maintaining a hierarchical structure that supports patriarchal dominance at all cost. Proponents of this argument believe that when parents abuse children they give up parental rights, and from that time forward they should not enjoy the privileges of parenting, which include the tempered use of power and control.

I consider these arguments simplistic and misinformed because systemic thinking is not a rigid formula applied indiscriminately; rather, it develops as a result of careful, individualized family assessments. If in fact a parent has gained a power hold on the family and demonstrates a pattern of abusive control, the family therapist will seek to diffuse the power hold and encourage the disempowered members of the family to regain personal power, safety, and control.

Disempowered family members include predominantly women and children, although there are many cases of child abuse in which women and girls exhibit dangerous abusive behaviors and boys and men are victimized. The same treatment principles—a speedy de-escalation of power-based behaviors and attempts to assist victimized family members to work on their own behalf to restore safety and control—would apply whether power was used abusively by a man or by a woman.

Treatment of abusive families is neither as complex or facile as it may seem. The abusive or neglectful behaviors are addressed in a focused way while contributing factors are constantly sought, identified, articulated, and addressed. Thus, treatment has a twofold approach: systemic interventions designed to address the climate that contributes to the emergence of abuse, and a variety of interventions directed at behavior, attitudes, and social/cultural factors. To illustrate the value of planning treatment services by using systemic thinking, I will present a case of sibling sexual abuse: the McGrath family.

The McGrath Family

Jason McGrath, a thirteen-year-old Caucasian youngster, was referred to treatment by his probation officer after molesting his ten-year-old sibling, Luann. Kristy McGrath called the police when she uncovered the fact that Jason had been molesting Luann for the past six months. Luann told her mother about the molestation in confidence, while Jason was away from home on a sports-related field trip.

Initially, Luann commented to her mother how much she

enjoyed the quiet since her brother's departure. Mrs. McGrath thought this comment unusual since Luann was very attached to her brother and in the past had missed him a great deal when he was away. She pressed Luann for specifics—that is, what was it about her brother being away that she enjoyed the most? Finally, Luann confided that she was sleeping better because she did not have to worry about Jason coming into her bed in the middle of the night and "bothering" her. Mrs. McGrath pursued a definition of "bothering," which Luann reluctantly described as Jason touching her genitals and inserting his finger into her anus and vagina.

When Mrs. McGrath called the police, she was distressed about what had happened in her family, and she was extremely irate with her son. Her comment, "They're all alike," was documented in the police report.

The police investigation was swift. Jason admitted the sexual abuse and seemed earnestly repentant. Although the case was referred to the district attorney's office by the police, Mrs. McGrath was encouraged to seek therapy for her son. Police officers noted that Mrs. McGrath was enraged at her son and had requested that he be taken out of the house and locked up as soon as possible.

When I met with the parents (Mrs. McGrath and Jason's step-father, Bill McGrath) it was immediately apparent that the mother had uncontrollable rage toward her son. She had sent him to stay with her brother because she could not stand to look at him. "I always knew he would do something like this," she asserted, and when I asked what made her think that, she recounted her own history of sexual abuse with tremendous insight and very little affect. She talked about her victimization as if she were talking about someone else. She was factual, yet disengaged from her feelings as she related years of sexual abuse. She described her father as "pathetic," "perverted," and "a degenerate," quickly adding, "like most men." She had been sexually abused from the time she was eight until she was sixteen; she had run away from home and married her first husband shortly after her sixteenth birthday.

Whenever I spoke to Mr. McGrath, her second husband, she quickly interjected her own answers to the questions. It soon became clear to me that it was important for her to be in control. When Mr. McGrath finally spoke, he deferred to her: "Those are her kids you know, and I'm just, well, a fill-in for their real daddy."

Mrs. McGrath discussed her former husband (the children's father) with great wrath, describing him as "lazy, no good, and a sexual pervert." When I asked why she used the term "pervert" she told me that he wanted to have sex all the time, "like most men," and he was disgusting.

When I asked about Jason, Mrs. McGrath was adamant that he was not welcome in her home, and that he needed to be put in jail. "Jail," she continued, "is the only thing that might straighten him out, God knows I've tried." When I asked what she meant by trying to straighten him out, she said that she had told him repeatedly that he was not to undress near, look at, or touch his sister in any way. When I asked her what made her warn him about those specific behaviors, she blurted out, "Boys are like that. They're born that way. Even when he was little, he was always trying to touch himself down there. I had to wrap his hands at night so he wouldn't touch himself. I also told him about my father and what he had done to me, and if I ever caught him doing anything like that to his sister, I would ring his neck." Apparently, mother had given both children explicit descriptions of her own sexual abuse in an effort to quell her fears about these events repeating themselves in her home.

Finally, I asked her where her own mother had been during the episodes of sexual abuse in her childhood, and she tearfully replied that her mother was physically disabled due to a car accident and spent most of her time in her own bed. "I only remember her a little before the accident, but I know after she got laid up she couldn't enjoy her life anymore, and she was always depressed, sad, on pain medications, or asleep."

Before she left I also asked her to tell me about both her children. Luann was painted as a charming, sweet, compliant, bright, friendly child. Jason was portrayed as the opposite: dull, mean, bothersome, and socially inept.

I considered this case within a systemic framework and realized that both parents contributed to the emergence of this particular symptom. First and foremost, the mother had a history of sexual abuse that was *unresolved*. She spoke about the incidents in a factual and disimpassioned way, as if the abuse had happened to someone else, not to herself. Her affect was not congruent with the events she described, which usually signals that the events have been kept compartmentalized and therefore not well integrated.

Segregating these conflictual experiences had not allowed her to process her feelings and obtain closure on the events. Consequently, the issues associated with her sexual abuse became pervasive within her current intimate relationships. Specifically, it was extremely critical for her to remain dominant in her relationships with men, because losing control represented danger. She therefore had selected compliant mates who did not challenge or threaten her dominant position. She had made numerous efforts to dominate her son as well, viewing his maleness as inherently perverted. Mrs. McGrath treated her children differentially: one child was identified as the problem, the other was the good child. She praised and validated her daughter while constantly humiliating and castigating her son. Consequently, it was easy to speculate that sibling jealousy might exist, and that Jason might harbor angry feelings toward his sister.

Jason's angry feelings became sexualized, in part as a result of receiving explicit information about what boys or men do to girls and women. His mother's attempts to prevent sexual abuse inadvertently contributed to a climate in which Jason merged sexual impulses with aggression, behaving in what his mother then viewed as predictable for males. Luann's victimization provided Mrs. McGrath with an opportunity to behave as a responsible mother, unlike her own mother, who was unable to stop the sexual abuse from reoccurring. I hypothesized that as the mother protected Luann and expelled Jason, she was addressing her own victimization and desire to be protected.

Mr. McGrath's role in this family is pivotal, in that his failure to confront or challenge his wife's beliefs about men contributed to the status quo. Not so coincidentally, Mr. McGrath had been raised in a physically abusive home in which his alcoholic mother had episodic violent outbursts. He had been unable to protect himself except by hiding until the violence passed. This vulnerability to explosive outbursts kept him compliant.

I was struck by his description of himself: "I pretty much stay out of everybody's way; I'm in the garage a lot." Had he been able to exert some control, to set limits on his wife's pervasive negative tone with Jason or in some way encourage her to feel safer around men who confronted her (without abusing her), perhaps some of the family dynamics might have changed. In addition, had he been more physically and emotionally available, Jason might have had an opportunity to establish a positive relationship with a male parent figure.

Using a systemic approach to treatment, it would have been futile to provide therapy to Jason without treating the rest of the family. It was the family's dysfunction that needed attention.

Initially, I offered Jason (who was placed in his uncle's home and did not go to juvenile hall) individual and group treatment, focused on sexual offender issues. In particular, he had many lessons to unlearn about male behavior, expression of anger, and so forth. I also saw Luann in treatment and although she was confused by her brother's behavior, it was her mother she was most concerned with. Apparently, Luann interpreted her mother's reaction to Jason as a statement that she (Luann) had done something wrong, and had hurt her mother's feelings. She was more troubled by her mother's rage, and by the absence of her beloved brother, than by the touching of her genitals, which she described as "not that bad. It tickled sometimes. He didn't hurt me and he wasn't mean to me." Luann often stated that she wished she had never told anybody what had happened.

I worked very intensively with Mrs. McGrath, first on her strong reactions to Luann, which she confused with her own thoughts and feelings about her victimization. She conceded that she had been disappointed that Jason was born a male, and had never felt motherly toward him. As she discussed her negative feelings toward her son, I inquired about her feelings about men in general, and eventually the discussion turned to her father.

It was fortunate that Jason was out of the home during the time that his mother worked on her childhood victimization, because her angry feelings exacerbated. Mr. McGrath almost fled the house completely during that period, choosing instead to make the garage his bedroom. As Mrs. McGrath began to redirect her anger toward her father in therapy sessions, and as she began to recall a positive relationship with her grandfather that she had virtually forgotten, her anger became less intense and was replaced with feelings of sadness and despair at the helplessness and isolation she had felt during the years she was sexually abused. Eventually, she acknowledged her anger and disappointment at her mother's inability or unwillingness to protect her.

Mrs. McGrath came to deal more effectively with her own sexual abuse, and this family-of-origin work preceded work regarding her current family.

I chose to refer Mr. McGrath to a male therapist to discuss his own abusive history, and he made great strides. I had met with him a few times and had sensed his discomfort in talking with me. He eventually confided that the fact that I was a woman in a position of authority produced great anxiety for him. I commended him on his courage in communicating this information to me, and referred him to a male colleague with whom he felt comfortable immediately.

Mr. McGrath's therapist and I together provided couples therapy to the McGrath's for approximately six months and we helped them function more effectively as a marital and parental team who could share responsibilities and make joint decisions. The process felt torturous to both of them at first, yet they both made a choice to invalidate their previous unspoken contracts and to establish new contracts between them.

Jason and his family remained in treatment for two years and Jason was successfully reunified with his family. Everyone seemed to benefit from individual and family therapy.

This example illustrates how a systemic view of the problem allowed me to develop a treatment plan that considered individual contributions, interactional problems (as fueled by family-of-origin issues), and problematic behaviors within all of the intimate relationships in the family. A nonsystemic clinician might have provided only individual and/or group treatment to Jason and/or individual and group treatment to Luann, which would have been insufficient and potentially dangerous.

Treatment Formatting

Continuing with the McGrath family as an illustration, I will further elucidate how a systemic approach strengthens the direction of treatment, in particular, decisions about who to see and in what order. Although I will discuss this issue generically later in this chapter, I will now summarize the guidelines I used to develop treatment plans for this family:

1. *Assess and treat individuals first.* In the McGrath family, I first interviewed each person separately, establishing a therapeutic relationship with each individual and listening to their particular perceptions of the problem. I offered the adults individual therapy, which Mrs. McGrath undertook and Mr. McGrath found uncomfortable. I referred him for individual therapy with a male colleague. I provided Jason with individual therapy and referred him to a group for youth who molest other youth. Luann was in treatment briefly, primarily to assuage her guilt about her perception that she had hurt her mother's feelings and caused her brother to be expelled from home.

Both parents had histories of childhood abuse that had created emotional vulnerabilities, patterns of interaction, and avoidant or phobic responses regarding important issues such as intimacy and power distribution in relationships. Jason's abusive behavior with Luann stirred up memories for each parent of his or her prior abuse and they both entered therapy to pursue these issues.

2. *Assess and treat subsystems as appropriate.* I met with the parents together to better understand how they functioned as a couple and as parents. I discovered that their relationship included a struggle for dominance and control, as well as a lack of intimacy. Mrs.

McGrath had failed to allow or encourage a parental role for Mr. McGrath, who kept his physical and emotional distance from everyone in the family.

The sibling subsystem was also conflicted since the children were treated differentially. Jason had cause to resent his sister since she received consistent positive attention from their mother, while Jason endured relentless negative attention from her. Precisely why Jason sexualized his anger is unknown, although his mother's explicit descriptions of her own victimization and the implied lessons regarding gender roles (males as abusers, females as victims), coupled with Jason's physiological changes brought on by puberty, probably contributed to his merging of sex with aggression.

3. *Offer therapy on marital/parenting issues.* Mr. and Mrs. McGrath participated in conjoint marital therapy to renegotiate their expectations of each other as spouses and parents. They developed more effective communication strategies and discussed and adopted a more cooperative partnership.

4. *Plan for family reunification.* Once Jason completed his treatment program for adolescents who molest siblings, he began a program of weekend visitations leading up to longer visits and eventual reintegration with his family. An "accountability session" allowed him to take responsibility for molesting his sister and to apologize to Luann for hurting her physically and emotionally. Subsequent family sessions dealt with rebuilding trust, establishing prevention strategies, and defining parental expectations of both children.

Figure 4.1 illustrates the progression from individual assessments and treatment to subsystem assessments and treatment (sibling, parental, and marital subsystems) and eventually to full family sessions.

Setting a Context for Change

Clinicians must create a safe and open environment in which difficult issues can be addressed, resistance can be overcome, and motivation for change can be elicited. Clinicians must find ways to help

FIGURE 4.1. The McGrath Family Treatment Format.

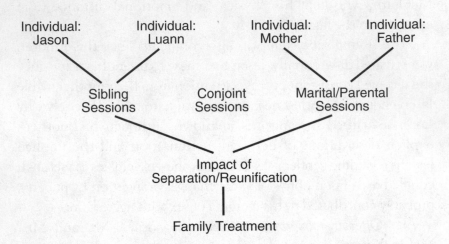

families from the very first contact, to encourage them to view the (imposed) therapeutic process as one that might have some positive consequences for them. Nothing motivates parental involvement (and decreases resistance) as much as having a rewarding experience of some kind.

The following exchange exemplifies the concept of being helpful as soon as possible. The interview occurred with a Caucasian mother of two who had been mandated to therapy because of physical abuse and neglect. The mother was angry at being forced to attend therapy sessions, which she perceived as irrelevant and a waste of time.

THERAPIST: I wonder if you might think of one thing that you think would help you at this very moment.

MOTHER: I can't think of a single thing.

THERAPIST: Take your time. See if you can pick one thing that you wish for, one thing that you think would make your parenting job a little easier.

MOTHER: What for? What's the use of hoping and wishing?

THERAPIST: I know. I know. It can feel pretty useless to hope and wish. But sometimes the only way we can get what we need or want is to figure out what it is first.

MOTHER: Well, I've been after my [social] worker about this for years, but I know if I could get the babies into day care during the day it might be a lot easier for me to get the job training and then get a job. Have you ever had to live on handouts? That's all welfare checks are—barely enough to pay the rent.

THERAPIST: So you would like to get your little kids into a day care program.

MOTHER: Yeah. And they've been promising me now for six months, and still there's no knowing when I can get them into that program.

THERAPIST: Okay, that's a reasonable request. If you have day care you can start your training program and hopefully get a skill that will get you a good job.

MOTHER: That's guaranteed. If I finish the program, they guarantee me a job as a welder.

THERAPIST: Do you know what the hang-up is?

MOTHER: Hell, no. They just keep playing hurry up and slow down. They don't care. It's no skin off their back if I go now or later. I'm just one little person. You should see how many people are on welfare. In their offices all you see are people waiting, waiting.

THERAPIST: I'm going to talk to your worker today and find out what the delay is. I can't promise anything, but maybe I can find out what the problem is.

MOTHER: Huh. If you find out, let me know.

THERAPIST: I will. I'll see what I can do. I really think you're making a reasonable request, because your goals are really worthwhile. Education, getting a job, getting more money coming in so that you don't have to worry all the time.

MOTHER: Yeah. Yeah. If I just didn't take one foot forward, two backwards.

THERAPIST: What do you mean?

MOTHER: I got accepted into the training program, then I got pregnant again.

THERAPIST: Oh.

MOTHER: I gotta be more careful.

THERAPIST: Are you practicing safe sex now?

MOTHER: The best kind of safe sex, no sex. I'm done having babies. I love my babies but enough is enough, I'll never get ahead.

THERAPIST: Kids can really slow you down.

MOTHER: Yeah, they can.

THERAPIST: I'll call that worker right after you leave today.

MOTHER: Hey, more power to you. Maybe you'll have better luck than me, but don't count on it.

The clinician may not always be in a position to get changes to happen, and he or she may be ineffective in obtaining needed additional information. However, clinical efforts to help in the client's real-life struggles are usually well received. Although resistant clients may take a wait-and-see attitude, clinicians can use these types of opportunities to become trustworthy and to be seen as tangible resources to help cope with real stressors. In the above example, the client stops short of expressing gratitude, but her anger and frustration seemed momentarily diffused.

Early in treatment, I anticipate resistance, respect it, avoid power struggles, and forge ahead with establishing myself as an ally rather than an extension of the referring agent (usually an authority figure). I believe that getting stuck in power struggles is one of the most common traps in treatment with nonvoluntary clients (the majority of families who abuse).

Because I anticipate that families will be angered or frustrated by being forced to participate in therapy, I usually make a remark early on that acknowledges this reality, such as "I am certain that you must have a range of feelings about being in therapy. Personally, I find it hard to do anything that is forced upon me, even when I know it's for my own good, like going to the doctor's or taking painful tests or such." In this way, I give permission for clients to volunteer their reactions to mandated treatment, and I also suggest that even though it may be painful initially, therapy might actually have remedial effects.

Convening Open, Multidisciplinary Meetings

More often than not, abusive or neglectful families perceive themselves as victimized by the system. This sense of victimization comes from the family's feelings of being forced to do something they don't want to do (attend therapy), being held accountable (to child protective services), feeling inadequate (at being told they've done something wrong), and being afraid (of being held legally accountable, as well as of the unknown and the possibility of children being removed from the home). The clinician's job is to help families regain a sense of control over their destiny, while at the same time addressing their abusive use of power or maltreatment of their children and helping to restore family safety and improved functioning.

Paradoxically, one of the ways to help families regain control is by inviting the participation in therapy of the very individuals they find oppressive—the system representatives who have been involved in filing or investigating child abuse reports. The purpose of such *open meetings* is to clarify expectations, clear the air, and help the family recognize that the therapy is not an extension of the law, but rather, a separate entity the function of which will be to assist the family to restore appropriate and safe functioning by providing them with specific alternatives to abusive or neglectful parenting approaches.

Open meetings are held after the family has met with the clinician to share their perception of the problem that has precipitated concern. The parents are told that the purpose of the open meeting is to achieve clarity, delineate roles, define exchange of information policies, and establish a treatment plan and format. Sometimes parents balk at the idea of talking in front of the very individuals they hold responsible for their fate, but other times they find such meetings to be an opportunity to defend or protect themselves. If that is the case, the family moves from being a passive to an active agent on their own behalf.

The clinician structures the meeting so that a chronology is established by professionals who have had contact with the family. In one such meeting, there were five professionals who had come into contact with the family: a schoolteacher, concerned by the child's bruises; a school nurse, who had examined the child several times during the school year; a school psychologist, who had conducted testing due to the child's sudden academic problems; a child-care worker, who supervised the child after school; and the social worker, who had been called by the teacher and who had interviewed the child at school about his bruises. As professionals take turns talking, they form a broader picture of overlapping concerns. The family is instructed to listen quietly, with the knowledge that they may make clarifying statements or ask questions before the meeting concludes.

During the next phase of the meeting, the family's current status is reviewed. For example, if the children are in custody, efforts are made to determine when case reviews will be held, how the decision to place was made, what the projected length of placement is, what visitation schedules are possible, and under what circumstances the children will be reunified with the family. The overriding concern in this phase of the meeting is to uncover specific expectations of the family, and to clarify the precise conditions for maintaining children in the home, or reunification.

The most critical task is to ensure clarity, so that treatment plans address the issues of concern to the clinician, the family, and the system personnel.

Once a chronology is established, the clinician helps to designate roles and delineate tasks, making sure that there is one person who serves as a case manager and liaison, to oversee the case in its entirety and maintain contact with the other professionals. This case manager may be the protective services worker, the schoolteacher, the therapist, or any other professional who is willing to coordinate services, call meetings, evaluate progress, and so on. These duties are usually within the purview of social services, and most often social workers function in this capacity. I have on occasion taken on the function of case manager myself because I felt that my rapport with the family ensured their cooperation, or because the social worker had such a large caseload that he or she could not provide the kind of attention needed. Clinicians should only do this, however, if they have the time and confidence to do so. Selecting a case manager decreases the chances of people functioning in a vacuum or assuming that others are fulfilling roles and functions that they are not.

It is very important that the clinician function as a devil's advocate, anticipating problems in the system's expectations and articulating options or alternatives to proposed solutions. In this way, the family begins to perceive the therapist as an ally. As the therapist structures the meeting and clarifies roles, duties, and direction, clients usually feel empowered and reassured by witnessing a goal-oriented and organized process.

The following exchange is from a multidisciplinary meeting in which the parent participated. I took every opportunity to establish myself as an advocate for the mother, who had been physically abused and terrorized and was experiencing lack of safety and ambivalence about protecting her child. This excerpt is taken from near the end of the session, when I endeavored to articulate social services' precise expectations of the mother. I directed my initial comments to the child protective services worker.

THERAPIST: You want to make sure that her husband is "out of the picture?" What happens if after she gets the restraining orders, and after she makes clear to him not to come around, he does anyway?

SOCIAL WORKER: Well, I think she needs to get the restraining orders, so he can't come near her house and can't get to the child at school.

THERAPIST: I'm just saying that this guy has a long history of breaking the rules. You know that. So, if he comes to the house in spite of the restraining orders, what do you expect she will do?

SOCIAL WORKER: She should call the police right away.

THERAPIST: Okay, and document that he's been there.

SOCIAL WORKER: Yes.

SOCIAL WORKER: And she shouldn't open the door to him.

MOTHER: I didn't *let* him in last time. He kicked the door down.

THERAPIST: I assume if he does something like that, you won't think mom is responsible.

SOCIAL WORKER: Not unless she's opening the door.

THERAPIST: That brings me to another point. You were checking into the possibility of her moving from the housing she's in now to another housing project that you think is a little more secure. What's happening with that?

SOCIAL WORKER: I tried to check with them before this meeting and no one called me back, but she is a high priority, and something might be available in the next few weeks.

MOTHER: Even if I move, he'll follow Dereck home from school and find out where we live.

THERAPIST: Well, that's a good point. To help her make as

clean a break as possible, and since there is a possibility of moving, any chance that Dereck can get transferred to a school closer to his new place, if that works out?

SOCIAL WORKER: I'm sure we can do that. This is also a per-fect time, because the school year's almost over. You could move during the summer, and then he could start in a new school.

THERAPIST: That sounds ideal. Does mom need to do any-thing about that now?

SOCIAL WORKER: I think she could find the public school for that neighborhood and maybe get some application forms for the fall.

MOTHER: I can do that.

THERAPIST: Now, one last thing. You've asked that mom and Dereck continue to come to see me, which they've said they will, and you are also requesting that she attend a battered women's group, is that right?

SOCIAL WORKER: Yes.

THERAPIST: Will victim's compensation continue to pay for Dereck's therapy and mom's therapy?

SOCIAL WORKER: Yes, and I'm sure the group work would be covered under collateral services.

THERAPIST: Okay, and do you want her to be in this group for any specific length of time?

SOCIAL WORKER: Whatever is available, and whatever you think might be helpful.

THERAPIST: So you're leaving that up to my discretion and what's available out there.

SOCIAL WORKER: Yes.

THERAPIST: So if she found a women's group that was meet-ing for twelve or fourteen sessions, that would be okay.

SOCIAL WORKER: Yes . . . and one more thing that we'll be looking for is that she stay in her job and establish a work record that's consistent.

THERAPIST: That's right. She hasn't done that before, mostly because of the beatings and having to stay out of work when she was injured. I don't think that will be happening anymore.

MOTHER: God willing.

THERAPIST: Well, God willing, and making all these changes to keep you and Dereck safe.

MOTHER: May I ask another question?

THERAPIST: Sure.

MOTHER: I'm very nervous about seeing him in court again for the sentencing.

SOCIAL WORKER: You don't have to be there for his sentencing.

MOTHER: I don't?

SOCIAL WORKER: No. I'll be happy to let you know what sentence he gets.

MOTHER: I'm still amazed that he's actually going to do some time.

SOCIAL WORKER: Your testimony was very strong.

MOTHER: I think the photos did the trick. I had no idea how badly hurt I was.

THERAPIST: You were very lucky to walk away without some major damage.

SOCIAL WORKER: I will need to have progress reports for Dereck.

THERAPIST: How about if I send you a copy of the progress reports that I send to Victims' Assistance?

SOCIAL WORKER: That will be just fine.

THERAPIST: [*To mother*] Are you quite clear on what Mrs. D. expects from you, and what she will be providing for you?

MOTHER: Yes, I think so.

THERAPIST: And if you have any questions come up, you know how to reach her?

MOTHER: Yes.

THERAPIST: [To social worker] Will you be visiting Dereck or his home?

SOCIAL WORKER: I'll probably drop in from time to time, but I feel good that we all know what each other is doing.

Developing Written Contracts

The therapist develops a draft of a written contract during the meeting, which is later typed up and sent for signatures. The therapist's primary concern while developing a contract is that professional expectations of the family be clearly set forward in exact behavioral terms. I have found that using written contracts prevents misunderstandings and maximizes the parent's compliance with agency or treatment expectations.

Developing Behavioral Objectives

Lack of specificity in the conditions set forth in a written contract can greatly compromise their value. For example, consider the vagueness of the following referral letter from child protective services:

Dear Dr. Gil: After an inconclusive investigation by our office we are referring the Smith family to you for treatment since we believe they have difficulty coping with their son's acting-out behavior and sometimes resort to extreme punishment of the child. We have advised the family that if their inappropriate behavior continues, we may file a dependency petition.

We are keeping this case open and look forward to hearing from you regarding their progress.

Although this letter provides basic information, it is not clear enough to establish a treatment plan with the family. I need to know, for example, what the investigation consisted of, in what way it was inconclusive, what the initial report stated and who made it, what acting-out behavior is difficult for the family, what child protective services considers "inappropriate behavior," under what circumstances they would consider filing a dependency petition, why the case is being kept open, and what type of information exchange they require from me, with what specific content.

In particular, when professionals use vague phrases such as "high-risk behavior," "inappropriate behavior," "harsh parenting," "seductive parent-child interactions," "improved parenting skills," or others, my first responsibility to myself and the family is to tease out a more exact definition so that there is clarity about what the treatment plan should address. For example, the phrase *high-risk behavior* may translate as leaving young children unattended, leaving one child in charge of another, not taking the child to medical appointments, or taking overtime without securing child care first.

Clinicians must ensure that goals and objectives are measurable. Exhibit 4.1 shows the objectives that would be listed under the goal "improve child care." Listing items in this way allows clients to maintain clarity about their high-risk behaviors, as well as to document their progress. Clinicians will also employ this list to gauge the family's focus and progress. Depending on the trustworthiness of the client's self-reports, clinicians may or may not need to get collaborating proof (that is, to check in with the physicians or get child-care workers to write weekly reports of their observations).

Written contracts are reviewed weekly and discussions are held regarding problem areas and perceived obstacles.

Exhibit 4.1.

1. Secure three new child-care resources

   Completed _____ Progress made _____

2. Keep an emergency fund for child-care expenses

   Completed _____ Progress made _____

3. Employ baby-sitters for both children so they are not left unattended

   # of times sitter used _____ # of times issue came up _____

4. Take child to medical appointments

   # of appointments kept _____ # of appointments missed _____

5. Accept overtime assignments only when child care is available

   # of overtime assignments taken with _____ without _____ child care

Writing the Document

A preliminary draft of the contract is discussed with the family at the next scheduled meeting. Clinicians and parents together finalize the language of the contract, which is then signed and submitted to other contractees (such as child protective services workers, police, probation officers, drug program personnel, and so forth). If specific conditions are included in court papers, these conditions should be clarified if necessary, operationalized, and incorporated into the treatment contract. Exhibit 4.2 contains a sample contract. The conditions set forth in this plan are specific and measurable. The parents know exactly what is expected of them if their children are to be returned to their care.

EXHIBIT 4.2.

This is a contract between _____ (parent[s] name) and
_____ (professional or agency) regarding the status of
_____ (children's names).

The current situation is that _____ are dependents of the court and reside in foster care due to a finding of physical abuse.

The following conditions must be met prior to the court's consideration of a reunification plan:

1. Father must participate in an inpatient substance abuse program for a period of time specified by the selected program.

2. Mother must participate in a parenting education class provided by community colleges, attending all classes, completing all homework assignments, and meeting all scholastic requirements of the course.

3. Parents must together write down a list of positive disciplinary techniques for toddlers, including a specific plan for toilet training they agree to follow, once discussed in therapy and approved by child protective services.

4. The family must participate in therapy as specified by Dr. Gil. The family must attend family therapy or couples therapy sessions as required and must cooperate fully with the treatment plan.

5. The children will participate in weekly therapy sessions with Dr. Gil and may eventually participate in family therapy sessions if and when reunification efforts are undertaken.

6. Parents agree to visit their children on specified every-other-weekend visitation schedules arranged with the foster parents.
Initial visits will be supervised by the foster parents.

7. Maternal grandmother will have weekly visitation visits, which she will arrange directly with the foster parents.

8. Therapist will write monthly reports to child protective services about the family's participation and cooperation with the court's conditions, specifying attendance or cooperation problems.

9. Parents will discuss with Dr. Gil any and all concerns regarding their ability to provide safe and nonphysical discipline to their children. Specifically, parents will bring up difficult or stressful parenting situations for clinical discussion so that appropriate disciplinary techniques can be identified.

Parent's Signatures _____ Child Protective Services _____
Date _____

Written Communications Between Agencies and Clinicians

Juvenile court personnel, lawyers, child protective services workers, probation officers, or the police often request updates on a family's progress in treatment. In particular, courts and welfare workers will require progress reports to develop recommendations about children's dependency status or ongoing need for protective action.

Clinicians often feel conflicted about sharing information about clients due to laws regarding the privileged communication between psychotherapists and clients. It is clear that the legal duty to report suspected child abuse supersedes the duty to maintain confidentiality, but less clear are the type and quantity of information that can legally be shared after clinicians begin treatment with abusive or neglectful clients. A good rule of thumb is to follow the same guidelines set up regarding the child abuse reporting duty, that is, to report knowledge or reasonable suspicion of abuse that elucidates the issues that caused the knowledge or suspicion. Likewise, once therapy begins, it is important to share information that continues to raise concern or suspicion as well as clearly established information such as attendance and cooperation.

It is possible for clients to attend all sessions and fail to cooperate with therapy. Clients can resist therapy by withholding information, disengaging from clinical conversations, or failing to complete homework assignments. It is also possible that some clients will "go along" with whatever they are asked to do or make temporary changes to appease professionals. This type of change is revealed by subsequent reports of ongoing difficulties by professionals who have contact with the children or parents.

Written reports allow clinicians the opportunity to clarify their perceptions of how therapy is progressing, which inevitably gives the family additional opportunities to alter their manipulative behavior.

Ordinarily, my reports to professionals are coauthored with the family and, if possible, signed by both myself and the parents. In this way the information exchange remains open, and families are less likely to feel that professionals are talking behind their backs or engaging in hidden agendas.

The content of reports is brief and includes a description of attendance and general cooperation with treatment. However, if clinicians experience family resistance or noncompliance, this is clearly stated. The following report was written with a couple who had physically abused and neglected their child. The child was in their custody.

> Mr. and Mrs. Lee have attended all scheduled therapy sessions; however, I have ongoing concerns about their participation in therapy. There are several items in our contract that have not been pursued, in spite of the fact that we have discussed ways to overcome obstacles.
>
> Specifically, they have been unable to attend stress-reduction classes and continue to report feeling physically fatigued and emotionally overwhelmed by job demands. Since both parents have been clear that it is when they feel under stress at work that they most perceive their child as a burden and feel resentful of his demands, it seems critical that they address the issue of stress reduction as quickly as possible. Although we have discussed specific behavioral approaches to stress, I have referred the parents to a class that teaches relaxation exercises and uses biofeedback techniques that are bound to be helpful to them.
>
> I find their unwillingness to follow through on this recommendation baffling and in contrast to their stated position that they wish to keep their child at home and will cooperate fully with treatment.

Writing this report and discussing it with the family encouraged them to express their ambivalence about therapy and their concern that "nothing would help" except better-paying jobs. They were apparently afraid to attend the stress-reduction class out of fear that it would not work and then they would have nothing more to try. Once these feelings were expressed, we were able to continue a discussion about how they could be more helpful to each other and get their attention and reassurance needs met both from each other and from their friends and extended family.

Avoiding Power Struggles

Disengaging from power struggles over alleged incidents of abuse or neglect is challenging. It is best to obtain available written information (such as child protective services or probation reports, court documents, and so forth) and to state the referral information that you have, asking parents to listen first and then to give you their account of what precipitated the referral, always avoiding struggles about "who done it." The following is a typical example of skirting power struggles. In this example, I am talking with an African American mother, whose husband hit their alcoholic son in attempts to get him to stop drinking. The father was unable to attend the session due to a car accident; much of what was discussed with the mother was later shared with the father.

MOTHER: This is the biggest misunderstanding I've ever seen. They've got the whole thing upside down.

THERAPIST: What I see in this police report is that someone came to your house and the child was huddled in a corner crying and stated that his father had hit him with his belt.

MOTHER: Well, yeah, but it didn't go down the way the police said it did.

THERAPIST: Tell me how it did go down.

MOTHER: What they didn't see is how James was mouthing off to his father, and the fact that he was drunk because him and his friends were off drinking again. That's the fourth time in the last six months or so he's come home drunk at dinner time.

THERAPIST: So you're both concerned about James and his drinking.

MOTHER: Yeah, he's a good boy most of the time. We think he's got some bad friends.

THERAPIST: So you're concerned about his drinking and about the kids he's hanging out with.

MOTHER: Yeah. And what are we supposed to do? You can't get through to these kids these days. Nothing else we do means anything to him.

THERAPIST: So you've tried other disciplinary techniques and they haven't worked.

MOTHER: Nope. His daddy's the only one who can get his attention.

THERAPIST: You mean when his dad uses a belt on him.

MOTHER: I didn't say he used a belt.

THERAPIST: Well, how does his dad get his attention?

MOTHER: When he gives him a whooping, but I'm not talking about child abuse.

THERAPIST: You mean his dad gets through to him when he uses corporal punishment.

MOTHER: Yeah. But only when James asks for it.

THERAPIST: And when does James ask for it?

MOTHER: When he's drunk and talks smart at his dad and me.

THERAPIST: So you mean that his dad has whooped him and then James has obeyed?

MOTHER: What do you mean?

THERAPIST: Well, you use a whooping because it gets his attention. Does that mean he stops doing what you don't want him to do?

MOTHER: Well, not really.

THERAPIST: So how many times have you whooped him to keep him from drinking?

MOTHER: Well, about three or four times.

THERAPIST: Then I guess it hasn't worked too well.

MOTHER: Well. . . .

THERAPIST: So mostly he's a good kid, but you get very worried when he's drinking and talks back at you and generally doesn't listen to you.

MOTHER: Yeah.

THERAPIST: Okay. So maybe what we can focus on in the therapy are ways to keep James from drinking and being disrespectful to you—ways that don't include whooping, because it doesn't sound like whooping works in the long run anyway.

MOTHER: Good luck.

THERAPIST: Yep, sounds like a challenge. Preadolescents are hard work, but three heads are better than one, or two.

In this example, the therapist obtains leverage by empathizing with the parent's point of view and identifying the issues that contribute to their abusive behavior. By allowing parents to talk about their concerns about their children and by expressing a willingness to focus on those things that are important to them, the parents' resistance is addressed. At the same time, the therapist sets a context for the work to be done, that is, the therapy will address the problems they have with their son, and attempts will be made to find other forms of discipline that don't include corporal punishment, since this, after all, has not been effective so far.

At this early stage in the treatment, I avoided arguments about whether or not a belt was used, whether or not "whoopings" constitute child abuse, and whether or not the father could be labelled "abusive." Later in treatment, there was ample opportunity to set limits on physical punishment, not only because there are other, effective ways to discipline and guide children, but because the parents had come to the conclusion that whoopings were not producing desired results.

Goal Setting

It is critical to define treatment goals as early as possible. I often summarize what I have heard parents say in the intake sessions, and convey to them my understanding of their problems and what I think I might be able to help them with.

To illustrate this process of defining goals, I will present the initial sessions with the Young family: Marge, Jack, and their daughter Tania.

When Marge called and asked me to see her daughter, Tania, I scheduled an appointment with all family members, although I often meet with parents first. In the first session, I asked Marge to tell me about her concerns regarding Tania, since she had made the initial phone call. I told Tania that this was her chance to listen and ask questions and later on she would have a chance to tell me as much or as little as she wanted. I also told her that we would have some time alone together in the playroom.

Marge reported that Tania was having trouble sleeping and often had nightmares. Her other major worry was that Tania seemed to spend most of her time alone and seemed to shy away from other children and fun activities. Marge noted that when she and her husband fought, Tania seemed worried, and that some women in her group had suggested she bring Tania into therapy.

Jack seemed interested in his daughter and reiterated Marge's concerns. "She seems to be, like, worried or something. Sometimes it's like she's scared of everything." When I asked both parents for their guesses about what might be worrying Tania, they both admitted that their fights became "loud," and that sometimes when things were not going well between them, they yelled at Tania as well.

Tania listened quietly and certainly fit her parents' description.

She played with some of the toys tentatively and sometimes disregarded them to pay close attention to her parent's words. In particular, when they talked about their arguments, Tania looked down and appeared sullen and still, hypervigilant and anxious. When I asked Jack and Marge to give me a better picture of what their arguments were like, Tania came over to her mother and asked to go to the restroom. She insisted that her mother accompany her. When they left the room, Jack changed the subject and I decided to forego the discussion until both parents were in the room. The next appointment was for the parents alone, followed by an appointment for Tania.

When the parents were alone I inquired further into their arguments and Marge reluctantly broached the subject of domestic violence. Jack interjected several minimizing comments, stating that his temper had been a problem "years ago," and that he had learned his lessons. Marge's descriptions belied Jack's minimization; she said he had slapped her across the face just three months earlier—"the last time," according to Jack.

Marge emphasized how she had begun attending a women's group after the last abusive incident and had found significant help from the program. She attended not only the women's group once a week but two or three meetings weekly of Adult Children of Alcoholics. Jack muttered that she had become a "junkie" and that perhaps Tania's worries stemmed from the fact that her mother was spending more and more time away from the house. "Maybe she's feeling scared that her mom's never home, ever thought of that?" he asked.

I took this statement as an opportunity to ask Jack about his feelings regarding his wife's new schedule. He shrugged his shoulders and said he didn't care. I waited patiently and he added "Well, sometimes I wish she was home more." Eventually he complained bitterly about having to fix dinners when he came home from work tired, and having to watch Tania. "Don't get me wrong, she's a great kid and all, but sometimes she just hangs around and asks a lot of questions. She seems to want a lot of attention. Sometimes I just want to sit and watch TV. I'm pooped after working all day."

When I asked each of them to describe their relationship with their daughter, Marge was enthusiastic but concerned, particularly over how the arguing (apparently the parents' euphemism for domestic violence) affected Tania. She stated that more than anything else she wanted to make sure the home was a "quiet" environment for her daughter. Jack apparently was less involved with his daughter and commented on her artistic abilities (he had once wanted to paint himself) and the fact that she was able to sit and watch football games with him, which he did not think most little girls would want to do or be able to do. Both parents felt the child was smart, did well at school, and had few friends or interests, preferring to stay home.

After this session, I summarized what I had learned about the family and made Jack and Marge a proposal for what I would do at that point. I asserted my concern for the domestic violence and verbal abuse that Marge had described. I also gave them my perception that their marriage was in crisis, which could allow them a great opportunity to reevaluate and redefine their relationship. It seemed like the couple wanted a cease-fire and was anxious to decrease the explosiveness and tension in their lives. I noted how it was Tania's anxiety that had alerted them to the seriousness of their situation, and I told them that Tania served as the barometer for their own anxieties and concerns. I told them that my guess was that Tania's hypervigilance had developed out of concern for her mother's safety and that she had learned ways to appease her father so that he wouldn't blow his stack.

I then revealed a preliminary treatment plan that consisted of individual therapy for both Tania and Jack as well as couples therapy for Jack and Marge. Since Marge was attending her women's group I felt it was not necessary for her to engage in individual therapy, but I said that if I changed my mind about that at a later time I would let her know.

The purpose of Jack's treatment was to get a handle on his volatility and contribution factors. In particular, I was interested in providing him with new strategies for handling his stress and anger. Since his way of releasing anger had been learned, I felt it was possible for him to learn new constructive and safe approaches to releasing tension.

I agreed with Jack and Marge that Tania appeared anxious and tentative and I planned to see her in play therapy sessions designed to give her a safe environment in which to bring these concerns to the surface and in which I could begin to help her work them through. I explained that play therapy was a way that children could use symbols (toys) to reveal their preoccupations, which might then allow me to facilitate a process of reparation. I expressed my optimism for the work we were about to undertake and commended them for taking the first step toward helping Tania with her fears and worries. Since I expected that her worries were tied in with the couple's patterns of domestic violence, it was important to address both dimensions concurrently.

This family treatment consisted of individual, couples, and family therapy sessions. In the family sessions the primary concerns were to make sure that individual goals were interacting successfully with family goals, and to hear from individuals about the progress they thought they were making. From time to time the overall treatment goals were articulated and redefined. Often in these sessions we used family play techniques to allow family members renewed opportunities to have positive and fun interactions. This family quickly replicated some of the family play activities at home and their together time became much more emotionally satisfying to all of them.

As you can see, in order to elicit the parents' cooperation with treatment, it is important to confront the problems of abuse and neglect directly, to create external controls until internal controls are utilized, and to offer a specific treatment plan that includes clinical reviews and revisions with family members.

Maintaining a Focus on Abuse Issues

It is not always easy to keep a focus on child abuse, particularly when parents seek to distract you, when there are ongoing crises to address, or when parents wish to communicate about unrelated issues that are less threatening and therefore easier to discuss.

One of the most useful things I have learned about being a therapist is to structure the therapy session immediately after clients take their seats. My supervisors always discouraged idle chit-chat and allowing sessions to wander aimlessly without setting a distinct agenda at the beginning of the clinical hour. I remember practicing the phrase, "What would you like to work on today?" and "What can I help you with today?" to cue clients to prioritize their problems and select topics they wish to discuss.

Since I have been working with abusive and neglectful parents, I have adjusted that phrase slightly so that I focus the clinical work through my question: "What issues regarding your children's safety would you like to discuss today?" or "What specific issues related to your abuse (or parenting) difficulties would you like to discuss today?" I also often ask about homework tasks from the week before, or say something like, "How was your week regarding the issues we talked about in the last session?" I might also ask if there are any specific concerns that arose during the past week regarding their children's safety. The clinical focus is thus directed to safety, and specifically, to issues of abuse or neglect. If the sessions are not structured in this way, it is possible for clinicians to collude with parental denial or ambivalence.

Following are excerpts from treatment sessions with the Young family (Marge, Jack, and Tania), introduced earlier, who had problems with both domestic violence and emotional child abuse. The excerpts are from both individual and family sessions, to demonstrate specific interventions such as maintaining a focus on abuse, observing family interactions, establishing external controls, treatment phasing and formatting, and termination issues.

Maintaining a Focus on Abuse.   The first excerpt is from an individual session with the father. Notice how it is difficult to stay "on track," which requires me to be focused and alert.

THERAPIST: So, how was your week?

FATHER: Man, I had a rough week.

THERAPIST: Tell me about it.

FATHER: Well, do you want to know about my hassles at work or at home?

THERAPIST: I want to know about anything that affected your ability to be a safe parent.

FATHER: Mostly I was okay with the kid.

THERAPIST: What about the rest of the time?

FATHER: I guess you'd say I had a little relapse.

THERAPIST: Describe "little."

FATHER: I yelled at them a few times, nothing too big.

THERAPIST: How did Tania react?

FATHER: She ran to her room.

THERAPIST: Then what happened?

FATHER: I did what you told me: I counted to fifty and then I went and apologized.

THERAPIST: Tania gets way too many apologies.

FATHER: I did what you said.

THERAPIST: Yeah, you did. You did what we talked about your doing if things get out of hand and you yell at her. But. . . .

FATHER: I know, I know, I'm not supposed to yell at her.

THERAPIST: Which I know is not easy for you.

FATHER: 'Cause sometimes stuff just comes pouring out.

THERAPIST: What stuff is that?

FATHER: You know. . . .

THERAPIST: Nope. I don't.

FATHER: The anger.

THERAPIST: What anger?

FATHER: The anger I got inside me.

THERAPIST: Oh, so it just spills out.

FATHER: Yeah.

THERAPIST: And you can't control it?

FATHER: I know I can, but sometimes I just can't get a hold of it.

THERAPIST: So up to now you haven't been too successful at catching it before it spills out?

FATHER: Nope . . . I mean Yeah.

THERAPIST: And it spills out on Tania.

FATHER: Yeah.

THERAPIST: Mostly it spills out on Tania.

FATHER: Yeah.

THERAPIST: How'd she get to be the one?

FATHER: The one what?

THERAPIST: The one you think it's okay to show your anger to?

FATHER: Well, her mom don't put up with it anymore [laughter].

THERAPIST: What does her mom do?

FATHER: She fights back. She won't take any of my crap anymore.

THERAPIST: So she can stop you more effectively than ever before.

FATHER: Yeah, it's not worth it to start up with her.

THERAPIST: Oh?

FATHER: She's told me that if I don't shape up she might just pack up.

THERAPIST: And your reaction?

FATHER: I don't want us to split up.

THERAPIST: So knowing there's a negative consequence, an external control, helps you not yell at her or hit her.

FATHER: Yeah.

THERAPIST: So your wife has learned how to get you to stop being abusive with her.

FATHER: Yeah, I guess you could say that.

THERAPIST: And what about Tania?

FATHER: Well, she, uhm . . . gets that little shy look on her face and won't say anything to me.

THERAPIST: And what does she do when you apologize?

FATHER: She's cool. After that, she just forgets about it.

THERAPIST: Do you think she really forgets about it?

FATHER: She doesn't say nothing about it.

THERAPIST: And does that convince you she's forgotten?

FATHER: I guess . . . I'm not sure.

THERAPIST: My guess would be she doesn't forget, she just wants her dad to stop being abusive.

FATHER: I don't know.

THERAPIST: What don't you know?

FATHER: I don't know. Tania's a good kid.

THERAPIST: I think so.

FATHER: I wish I didn't get so pissed off at her sometimes.

THERAPIST: So do I. That's what we're here to work on: how

come it is that she's the one you yell at when you feel bad about work, or money, or anything else. It's almost like she gets the worst and the best of you.

FATHER: Yeah, that's true.

THERAPIST: She also can't fight back. When you feel helpless and angry at other people you feel you can't tell them, but you'll tell Tania instead. With her you feel power because she can't fire you, or fight back, and she forgives you almost immediately. At least it seems that way.

FATHER: Well, she does forgive me. She tells me so.

THERAPIST: But that doesn't mean she forgets how afraid she feels, or how you hurt her feelings.

FATHER: I guess not, but still, she's a trooper.

THERAPIST: Why? Because she takes it quietly.

FATHER: Takes what?

THERAPIST: Your abuse.

FATHER: No, I mean she's my little girl. She loves me and she's always happy to see me. She just puts up with me better.

THERAPIST: Better than who?

FATHER: Better than anybody else.

THERAPIST: What do other people do?

FATHER: I don't know. You know, get pissed, or . . . I don't know. If I ever told my boss what I thought, he'd can me quicker than I could say "I didn't mean it."

THERAPIST: So, there are consequences to your abuse with other people. But Tania can't fight back. She becomes your favorite target because she's little and can't stop you. I want to make sure that you know that it's not okay to yell at her and scare her and that your apologizing doesn't make it all better or wipe it away.

FATHER: I know that. I felt bad about it.

THERAPIST: When?

FATHER: When she went to her room.

THERAPIST: I want you to feel bad about it before she goes to her room, before you let loose on her. [*Pause*] So you stopped being abusive with your wife Marge because of something she does.

FATHER: Well, yeah.

THERAPIST: And you wouldn't think of spouting off at your boss because you'd be fired.

FATHER: Probably.

THERAPIST: So it's like you're telling me that you can control yourself when others set consequences on your behavior. [*Father looks confused.*] Well, you don't yell at your boss because he'll fire you and you don't yell at Marge anymore because she will stop talking to you for weeks.

FATHER: Yeah, that's true.

THERAPIST: It sounds like you can stop yourself when you want to.

FATHER: I guess so.

THERAPIST: And now I want you to figure out a reason why you would stop yelling at Tania.

FATHER: Well, I do get mad at lots of other people.

THERAPIST: Yeah, but just Tania gets the flood.

FATHER: What flood?

THERAPIST: The one that spills over.

FATHER: Oh, yeah. I guess you could say that.

THERAPIST: That's how you describe it—you can't control it, it spills out.

FATHER: Yeah.

THERAPIST: But in fact you can control it. When you want to. When you see a reason to do so.

FATHER: I guess.

THERAPIST: So how does this well fill up so much that it spills out?

FATHER: It's a mighty deep well.

THERAPIST: Deep, eh? How long does it take to fill?

FATHER: Not too long when I'm at work.

THERAPIST: So it fills up at work and spills out at home.

FATHER: Yeah.

THERAPIST: How come it doesn't spill out at work?

FATHER: I told you already. If I let loose at work, I'd get canned. Remember that guy I told you about a few months ago, Joe, the guy with the temper?

THERAPIST: Yeah. He spilled out at work like you do at home.

FATHER: That's the one. He's gone now.

THERAPIST: Well, I'm just wondering, if you had a well, and it rained buckets and the well filled up, and it spilled over, and it overwatered the garden, and the roots rotted out and the flowers died, what would you do?

FATHER: I don't know.

THERAPIST: Well, think about it. Apparently the spilling over is a problem. What would you do?

FATHER: I guess I'd think about a bigger well.

THERAPIST: OK, that's an idea. What else?

FATHER: I guess, maybe figure out how to drain it.

THERAPIST: Drain what?

FATHER: The well?

THERAPIST: Oh.

FATHER: Or figure out how to use the excess water in some other area, like maybe start another garden and get long hoses so that the water could be put somewhere else where it was needed.

THERAPIST: And where it wouldn't do harm to the flowers.

FATHER: Yeah.

THERAPIST: Okay, so let's talk about draining.

FATHER: You mean at work?

THERAPIST: You got that really fast.

FATHER: I just don't know how to go about it.

THERAPIST: The problem is that you have only had one option: the well fills up and it spills over. You see how that's just one solution.

FATHER: Yeah, as opposed to the draining.

THERAPIST: So, when I asked you at the beginning about what you wanted to work on, the spilling over is one problem, and it was great you could apologize to Tania so she knows she's not the problem, but I think the other problem is equally important, and that is how to keep that well from filling up to the spill point, and how to drain it properly.

FATHER: Yeah, I guess that's where I need work.

THERAPIST: So we've got to figure out how your well fills up, how you let it accumulate, and how to keep it from spilling over on Tania.

FATHER: I get it.

The father provided a metaphor for discussing his feelings of anger building up and accumulating into explosive outbursts. There are several important discussion points in this conversation, such as his relationship with his spouse and her setting limits effectively, and his ongoing exploitation of his daughter. It was important to point out that he was using an external locus of control, and yet inevitably he was the one choosing when and how to let out his anger and under what circumstances to keep his angry feelings to himself. It was also important for him to perceive the exchanges with his daughter in a different way. As long as he rationalized that she was unaffected by his angry outbursts, he continued to behave in an abusive manner with the expectation of quick forgiveness. He needed to understand that just because Tania said she forgave him did not mean she forgot the abuse easily or was not affected by it.

During this meeting, Mr. Young and I spent some time on the stress buildup he described at work and we discussed what he could do with his angry feelings before they accumulated and "spilled out." In his own childhood he had been physically abused and had therefore learned that anger could only be handled in one of two ways: either you hold it in (which he did at work), or you release it in an abusive way (which he did at home). He did not know that it was possible to communicate angry feelings in a nondestructive fashion, or to use anger to clarify concerns that could then be examined in a constructive way. We role played a number of different ways he could approach his boss and coworkers, and although he felt awkward and made no promises about trying out these new interactions, he was interested in the possibilities.

Therapy had helped this father become more aware of his problem. When he was verbally abusive to his daughter he apologized. Tania knew from family therapy sessions that his apologies were his way of letting her know that he was working on his problems but that they did not make him less accountable for his behavior. I was clear with him that his verbal abuse was not acceptable and I framed it as a relapse that showed there was still more work to do. This session demonstrates the importance of keeping the focus on abuse and safety issues.

Observing Family Interactions.   Concurrently with the father's individual therapy, I saw Jack, Marge, and Tania in family therapy sessions. It was of particular importance for me to have the opportunity to observe parent-child interactions, because I have learned in the course of my work with abusive or neglectful parents that family members' descriptions of interactions are often incomplete or distorted and must be supplemented with direct observations.

I also saw Tania in individual play therapy sessions. Tania was a pseudomature, hypervigilant, compliant ten-year-old child, whose primary concern was pleasing those around her. She was one of the few children I have seen who was preoccupied with cleaning up the playroom before leaving and who often asked how my day was or whether I was feeling tired. It was clear to me that she was a child who had lived in an inconsistent and explosive environment. She was adept at scanning the environment for signs of distress or disapproval. She had remarkable caretaking abilities, which I assumed had developed as a result of caretaking her mother in past years.

Tania and Marge had lived in a physically and emotionally abusive and threatening environment. Marge had been physically abused a few times over the years; the physical abuse was erratic enough to present a clear danger and keep her disempowered. At the same time, because it never developed into a predictable pattern, Marge claimed it allowed her "recoup time" in between beatings, and gave her a chance to "get myself focused on what to do next."

Marge was lucky in that she had been able to break out of the abusive pattern by seeking help for herself. She called the women's group she had joined her "salvation." It was shortly after she had joined the group that she brought Tania for therapy, because the group had encouraged her to see that Tania was a victim as well, in spite of the fact that her husband had never hurt Tania physically.

Tania had been Marge's confidante and caretaker. During the day, while Jack worked, Marge was often depressed and stayed in bed watching television. Sometimes she kept Tania at home with her so she had company and did not feel so lonely. Tania had learned to take care of her mother well, often combing her hair, washing and ironing clothes, and fixing meals. Tania had also learned to fix dinner for her dad, and try to appease him so there would be no explosive outburst when he arrived home at the end of the day.

As Marge became more functional, things got worse for Tania. Marge was frequently out of the house when Jack arrived home, and as Jack indicated, Tania would often receive the brunt of his anger. He had never struck Tania, but he often used words to belittle and humiliate her. He was quick to beg her forgiveness and would often hold her in his arms and rock her during ritualized acts of contrition. Tania described her "nice" and "mean" daddies as if they were separate persons. She loved her nice daddy tremendously and described laughing with him, playing with him, and his reading stories to her while she sat comfortably in his lap. The mean daddy was loud, scary, and had mean eyes. When he was around, she went to her room and pretended to be asleep. She never cried, though, because she did not want to hurt her nice daddy's feelings.

In family therapy sessions, the family's situation was made explicit: Marge had become empowered through her therapy, Tania was often left alone to cope with her father's moods, and Jack felt committed to working on his abusive behavior, but often "slipped" with Tania. In addition, the parents were negotiating their marital relationship and seemed motivated to redefine and solidify their relationship. The first nine years of their marriage had been "enjoyable and peaceful," and they both felt they had a good history to build on.

In the earlier family therapy sessions, I got a firsthand view of how Tania arbitrated the contact between her parents and how she behaved around her father's volatility. During one particular session, I had each family member draw a picture of "you and your family doing something together." Marge drew a picture of the three of them sitting down to dinner, Jack drew a picture of a picnic by a lake (he floated in the lake on an inner tube while Marge and Tania slept under a tree), and Tania drew a picture of her mom and dad in bed, with her bringing in breakfast on a tray.

When they finished making their pictures, I asked them to show them to each other and say a little about what was going on in the pictures. Jack's picture was first, and he jokingly talked about how everyone in his picture was tired and needed to rest. Marge cajoled him about a time when he had fallen asleep on an inner tube and gotten second-degree sunburns; both parents provided vivid descriptions of that outing to Tania, who seemed delighted at her parents' pleasant exchanges.

When Marge showed her picture, Jack made a provocative statement: "I can't believe you remember us sitting down to dinner. When was the last time the three of us had dinner together, huh?" Marge reacted to the statement by picking herself up from the circle on the floor and sitting on the chair behind her. "You're such a jerk," she said, "You always have to ruin everything." Tania immediately stood next to her mother, holding her hand while placing herself between mother and father.

Jack remained on the floor. "Oh, for Christ's sake," he said loudly, "do I have to censor every little thing I say? Can't you take a joke?"

Tania looked at her dad and with a very small, pleading voice and said, "It's okay daddy, don't be mad, she didn't mean it." Marge took her daughter's hand and said, "Honey, don't worry. Your dad is mad at me, not you. Nothing bad's going to happen." Jack got up and sat across from me. "Doesn't this take the cake? You heard what I said. All I said was the truth, and she gets bent out of shape about it."

This was a perfect opportunity to observe the family's most prominent response to the sudden threat of violence. Tania became protective of her mother; Marge tried to reassure Tania, and Jack felt left out and misunderstood.

I chose to keep interventions to a minimum and encouraged them to work things out between them. One of the first things Jack did was apologize to Tania. Tania quickly grabbed her picture and tried to talk about it as if wanting the negative feelings to be forgotten quickly. The parents allowed her to do so, and I noted that it was as if the issue had been swept under the rug, and now there was a big bump under the rug that people might trip on.

I asked Tania if she remembered what had just happened, and she quietly agreed she did. Then I asked the parents if there was some way they could resolve the issue in such a way that it did not get swept under the rug so quickly but rather got discussed and ironed out before it got put away. They agreed and once again tackled the specifics of the incident, alternately withdrawing and attacking. I helped the parents describe the feelings that provoked their responses, and they both talked about feeling hurt and misunderstood. Eventually, both Jack and Marge apologized for being insensitive and claimed to understand each other's reactions, although I wondered how superficial or deep their understanding of each other truly was.

Tania then got a chance to describe her picture and it was clear to everyone how hard Tania worked on unifying her parents and taking care of them. In a show of great sensitivity, father and mother agreed to serve Tania her favorite breakfast in bed the following morning.

Creating External Controls. When working with abusive and neglectful parents it is helpful to conceptualize individuals whose internal controls are not functioning for a variety of reasons. Abusive and neglectful behaviors are perceived as "just happening out of the clear blue," or as happening when "something comes over me." Most abusive parents describe feelings of lack of control, explosiveness, or chaos. It is highly unusual to work with abusive parents who plot and plan how to hurt children, unless they are sadistic abusers who feel satisfied, fulfilled, aroused, or made powerful by children's pain. Most of the time, parents are only referred to treatment when an evaluation reveals the possibility that they might be helped.

As discussed in Chapter One, an array of factors contribute to child abuse and neglect, although there is rarely a single, linear cause and effect. Although poverty can contribute to stress, frustration, anger, and violence, not all poor people abuse their children, so poverty can be seen as only one of many contributors. Likewise, although the need for power usually underlies an adult's sexual exploitation of children, some parents who sexually abuse are just as driven by the need for closeness and unconditional love and acceptance, and by feelings of inadequacy.

One of the earliest clinical tasks is to ensure that a range of external controls are in place to assist in maintaining children's safety during the course of therapy. External controls are imposed to set definitive limits on abusive or neglectful behaviors. They can be enacted by numerous professionals in a variety of different ways. For example, parents might be required to take their child to a pediatrician for weekly or monthly exams so that an independent person can ensure that the child is not being physically abused. Clinicians might alert parents to the possibility that a new child abuse report will be filed under certain circumstances. The threat of children's removal or conditions for returning children to the home might dictate specific actions that can be evaluated.

Clinicians may encourage children to disclose specific behaviors about the family. Placing the responsibility of monitoring on children is problematic, but may often be a reliable source of valuable information. Teachers also may be asked to report on children's attendance or on their comportment in the school. Sometimes extended family members can be contacted to provide feedback about the family's situation. The family is always informed in advance of such monitoring and any negative reactions are discussed at that time. If family members view these external controls as necessary on a temporary basis, they might even be well disposed to altering their behavior to achieve the desired results.

The potential danger of utilizing external controls is that someone will alter their behavior as long as the controls are in place, but the behaviors will be abandoned once they achieve their goals. The challenge of treatment is to encourage attitudinal changes that might reinforce the value of the new behaviors. In other words, the hope is that if people can alter their behavior because of an external control, they might recognize the value of the change and incorporate it on a long-term basis.

For example, Jack initially altered his abusive behavior with his wife out of a realization that she might dissolve the marriage and separate from him, a negative consequence he wished to avoid. Eventually he reevaluated his angry outbursts and found them useless and counterproductive. He committed himself to learning other ways of dealing with his emotions and practiced a variety of new techniques that he found kept him from feeling enraged and helpless.

Jack also learned an interesting lesson about his relationship with his daughter. As she felt more confident that he would not explode, she allowed herself to behave in a more relaxed manner around him. As she showed herself more fully, he was able to get to know her better and found that they became better friends. He realized that his daughter had needed to protect herself from him and his angry outbursts. He also acknowledged that her shyness was really fear and he painfully recognized that he had contributed to her general anxiety.

Although Jack initially altered his behavior to avoid a negative consequence, he eventually recognized that his behavior had caused his wife and child great pain and anxiety. He also found that his anger had allowed him to feel helpless in his job setting and contributed to his feelings of frustration and dissatisfaction. As a result of his insight, he committed himself to processing his anger in a different way, and to reconnecting with his child and wife in an enhanced way.

Keeping the System Open.   Abusive and neglectful families tend to be isolated; family members often depend exclusively on each other and are unable to form fulfilling relationships with others. This interdependence can lead to exclusionary or protective behaviors, particularly on the part of the parents.

Jack and Marge, for example, saw few friends and kept to themselves. Marge confided that early in their relationship they were much more social and enjoyed other couples' company. "Nowadays," she reported, "we shy away from seeing other people." She thought this change was related to wanting to avoid explosive outbursts in front of their friends or extended family.

"We just stay to ourselves now, and even Tania seems to want to hang around the house." In the individual therapy sessions, Tania's play was repetitive. She often had a girl doll spending time with her mother and father, bringing them coffee, washing their clothes, even giving them backrubs. The little girl sat up in bed at night listening for "noises." She would go to sleep only after the mother and father doll had done so. Tania volunteered that the little girl in her play "lived to make mom and dad happy," and she could not leave them alone because "they might get mad and say mean things to each other."

Tania's pseudomature and anxious behavior was a direct result of the fear she felt about the possibility that her mother would get hurt by her father, or that the family would "break apart." Marge's isolation was self-imposed but equally protective. She was concerned that others might see Jack's volatile behavior and she was ashamed by her inability to change things for herself or her family. Jack seemed content to keep social commitments to a minimum and described himself as "tired and irritable. I would much rather stay at home and watch television than do much of anything else."

One of my goals with the Youngs became to create more flexibility in this isolated family that often felt alienated from others who had it "better," or "easier." The easiest place to begin was with Tania, and with helping the parents find an age-appropriate activity for her. Both parents liked the idea of art classes, since Tania often drew for hours. Tania was ambivalent about attending classes. She seemed excited to go once her parents told her that they planned to go to a bookstore to browse while she attended classes. The bookstore was nearby and both parents told Tania how much they liked to look around in bookstores and how happy they felt to have a chance to do so.

Tania seemed willing to attend her classes, yet she had a number of excuses for missing them. The family and I had discussed Tania's ambivalence about participating in age-appropriate activities and the parents anticipated her resistance, simply staying firm about taking her to her class each time. Tania came back from class overjoyed to have spent time doing one of her favorite activities and she was proud to show off her countless art projects.

Jack and Marge next discussed something that the two of them could do together outside the home. It turned out that they had met while on opposing bowling teams and that they had enjoyed this sport quite a lot in their earlier years together.

Jack had great difficulty finding an evening in which he could come home from work early. Marge did not have as hard a time, but the couple did negotiate for quite a while about the specific night they would reserve for each other. Eventually, they got into a routine and found that they enjoyed not only each other's company but other friends with whom they bowled. The bowling routine was interrupted once when Marge and Jack had a fight about how the scores were recorded. Jack had implied that Marge's approach was "faulty," and she had become irate and embarrassed by him. They raised this issue in therapy and resolved it to some satisfaction; they both agreed to approach each other with suggestions in a more private fashion.

Marge was pleased with Tania's newly acquired social skills and decided to bring Tania to a child-care situation that was available while she attended her women's group. Apparently there was an opportunity in this situation for children to talk about school, parents, chores, and other relevant issues and Tania made her first "best friend" from this activity.

The family responded well to the treatment goal of opening the family system and gradually made efforts to expand their experiences and turn to others for conversation, companionship, or support.

When I am working with abusive or neglectful families, another consideration is expanding the family system beyond friends and family to community contacts as well. For example, I encouraged Marge and Jack to talk with Tania's teacher to find out how she was doing in school. I also encouraged them to maintain contact with her art teacher, as well as the child-care worker at Marge's group meetings. Not only is it useful for parents to engage actively in their children's lives, but this type of contact allows for greater professional involvement in the family's life, which is particularly neces-sary during stressful times. Especially when the focus of the work is children's safety, the more professionals I can talk with regarding a child's progress, the better. This extended professional contact cre-ates a protective environment that surrounds the child and her fam-ily—somewhat like a protective net that then remains in place and is valuable when designing protective efforts in the future.

Formatting Issues.   As I stated in Chapter Two, my preference is to start with individual assessments, partly because family members who are dealing with abuse issues are by definition stressed out, in pain, and in crisis, and tend to feel alienated from each other. They may therefore behave toward each other in inappropriate, hurtful, or demeaning ways. Such behavior is particularly salient when meeting with children and their parents together. One argument in favor of beginning with family sessions is that children have prob-ably heard their parents' insults or accusations prior to attending therapy and therefore are not affected by it. However, if a thera-peutic alliance is not established separately with parents, the clini-cian may find it more difficult to set limits on inappropriate parental behaviors. It is more likely that parents will follow clinical direc-tives after they have had a chance to establish a respectful and trust-ing relationship with the therapist.

In addition, if it is a child's allegation that has resulted in the family being referred to treatment, early family sessions can deteri-orate into cross-accusations of wrongdoing or a child's submission into silence. For these reasons, I believe that in most cases it is more effective to have full family sessions after individual sessions are conducted.

Colleagues ask this question consistently: Should a single clin-ician attempt to see all family members, including children, or is it better to have more clinicians involved? I learned early in my train-ing that rigid policies are limited and ineffectual. In one of my internship programs, the child therapists could only work with chil-dren; parents were seen by another therapist, and the chances of joint sessions were pretty slim. As an intern, my requests to see parents or families was viewed as provocative. To this day, I think about some of the children I worked with, mistakes I made (see Chapter Six), and how restrictive it was to adhere to policies that I now perceive as imposed due to budgetary rather than clinical concerns.

Currently, my best advice to clinicians about how to decide who to see in a family is to make a realistic assessment of one's own skills and time availability and of the complexity of the case. For example, if a clinician is equally conversant with child therapy, couples therapy, and family therapy, he or she can probably structure the treatment as a single therapist. In addition to evaluating one's clinical skills, it is important to recognize how much time is involved in providing individual, couple, or family therapy to all family members, and to remember that the therapy can be staggered so that individual therapy is followed by couples work, or conjoint sessions may be scheduled.

Lastly, clinicians should consider the type of problems involved and whether they would benefit from working in a clinical team. Just as they must evaluate their own skills as a child therapist or couples therapist, clinicians must also recognize their limitations in content areas. A therapist might feel well trained to work with child victims of child abuse, but unfamiliar with sex offender treatment or treatment of violent individuals. In this case, the clinician might consider referring the client to someone with that expertise and coordinating the treatment plan with that person. In some work settings, a group of clinicians are available to provide specific types of services, so even though a referral is being made, the case is being kept "in-house," and the clinician will have the benefit of working with a close colleague.

I cannot say enough about how complex and taxing these cases can be, and more often than not I prefer to work in a team context with a co-therapist. Not only does working together relieve the pressures inherent in working with child abuse, it also helps the family to learn from safe and nonthreatening interactions between a co-therapy team, and it allows clinicians to buffer the burden of making critical life-and-death decisions by offering joint opinions.

Treatment Phasing.   Since the overriding goal is to stop the abuse and make certain that the children are safe, all clinical interventions revolve around this intent. The greatest priority is to provide necessary help to the child or person who has been injured emotionally or physically, to restore or enhance the nurturing and protective capacities or abilities of the nonabusive parent, and to give immediate and concrete help to the person who has abused.

Most abused children benefit from play therapy experiences, which provide them with a secure, nondemanding environment in which they can play freely and address their worries and concerns in a variety of nonverbal and verbal ways. The length of this treatment depends on the child's idiosyncratic response to the abuse, and on the extent of the damage incurred. Play therapists conduct comprehensive evaluations designed to uncover developmental concerns as well as affective or behavioral problems.

Nonabusive parents likewise benefit from individual therapy, which often attempts to review and elucidate the circumstances leading to the emergence of abuse within a family. Historical information, significant developmental events, childhood experiences with violence or nurturing, mate selection, how the decision to have children was made, and other relevant factors are obtained. Clinicians can then create treatment plans based on the individual's current needs.

Individuals who abuse or neglect require specialized services that provide education, attempt to eliminate or remove obstacles to change, address cognitive distortions, and take great care to provide alternative behavioral responses to precipitating issues. In addition, most individuals who abuse require structure and monitoring; the most effective context in which to provide sex offender therapy, for example, is one in which the individual attends therapy and reports to probation or serves a sentence.

Contracts must be reviewed every two months. The clinician

and the family need to verify that the focus has been maintained and that progress is being made. If items need to be renegotiated, it is important to do so immediately. I also find that clients benefit from keeping ongoing documentation of what works and what doesn't work for them. These records can be periodically reviewed in and out of treatment. New behaviors need to be reinforced often and explicitly. Clinicians should take every opportunity to verbalize any forward movement in their clients, no matter how small, comparing and contrasting the old and new behaviors.

Termination.   I know I can begin the process of termination when my records indicate that clients have cooperated, issues have been addressed, behavioral changes have occurred both in and out of therapy, and family interactions appear to have improved based on individual and collective reports.

Certain changes are qualitative rather than quantitative, including what I can best describe as hope, optimism, self-confidence, and feelings of positive self-regard. These changes are demonstrated physically as well as verbally. Both adult and child clients begin to hold their bodies more upright, to walk with an air of self-assurance, to take controlled risks, to make future-oriented statements (such as "when I get older," "when I have another relationship"), and they seem to take pride in their achievements. They also report feeling closer to their family, and feeling more open, receptive, and responsive to others.

I always talk openly to people about termination, reviewing their progress and proposing a plan for decreased meetings and a termination date. On occasion, as with other, generic clients, clients will take small steps backward, but in the context of termination resistance, those steps can be viewed and explained as behavioral objections to ending what has been a positive therapeutic relationship.

One termination intervention that I always use is a series of sessions that review the past, the present, and the future. During these family sessions, each person is asked to say what has changed about him- or herself since right before the abuse happened. A child might say, "I used to be scared of talking back then." A nonabusive parent might state, "I was really depressed then and I frankly didn't like being at home. When I was there, I was in my room." A parent who abused might offer, "Drinking is not an excuse, but I had lots of frustration that I tried to avoid by getting drunk and passing out. The more I drank, the more I hated myself. I need to stay on top of my drinking, but more importantly, to deal with the stuff that made me want to drink in the first place." I like everyone to have a clear idea of what was going on prior to the abuse, and I then label those "red flags," which must be carefully monitored.

We then move to the present, and everyone discusses the changes he or she has made or the lessons that have been learned or integrated. The focus on the future involves not only what growth they may still wish for, but what specific resources they have available should problems or concerns arise anew. This focus on prevention is usually empowering for the family, and reassuring to me.

Formulating the problem of child abuse within a systemic framework allows clinicians to consider individual and collective family needs. Setting a context for change requires the clinician to be helpful in a concrete way, to address resistance, and to elicit internal motivation to change. Setting a context includes becoming trustworthy in word and deed. I therefore make efforts to posture myself as an ally, distinguishing my roles and responsibilities from those of other professionals involved in the case. In addition, I convey the message that people are entitled to feel ambivalent or angry about being forced to attend treatment. Initially, I avoid any and all power struggles, making special efforts to empower the family in whatever way possible, since they arrive in treatment in a one-down position. As parents begin to view me as an ally, resistance decreases naturally.

Unexpectedly, I have found that convening open, multidisciplinary meetings provides me with an opportunity to champion my clients' case, clarify agency expectations, and anticipate potential problems and solutions. During multidisciplinary meetings, which parents attend, I define and list what is expected from the family, who will provide such services, and who will oversee the case.

In addition, to further establish myself as trustworthy, I only communicate with referring or protective agencies through reports that are coauthored with my clients. This process appears to have a calming influence on families, who feel a restoration of power, as well as a sense that their voices are respected and heard.

Written contracts allow clients to follow directives toward their desired goals. A parental goal may be to keep the child from being removed form the home, but the contract goal will specify the actions or behaviors—the treatment goals—that must occur in order to meet the parents' goal.

As a consultant in the area of family violence, I urge clinicians to crystallize their plans, review them periodically to see if necessary changes are occurring, and to remain flexible to formatting options based on family responses. In addition, prioritizing treatment needs with a focus on safety, ensuring external controls, making direct observations, and reinforcing new behaviors are important elements of this work.

Termination is undertaken the same way treatment is begun, with a clear explanation of what the clinician sees and understands, with a plan for decreasing clinical contact, and with a review of available support services for the future.

5

Assessing Family Readiness for Reunification

with Monica Roizner-Hayes

As discussed in Chapter One, one of the unique factors inherent in treating families who abuse is the probability that the clinician will be asked for professional opinions regarding profound issues such as when and if children should be separated from or reunited with their parents; how to determine if an abusive parent has truly changed; what the effect is on victims of living with parents who were once abusive; how long children can be kept in a foster care system unable to secure permanency; and when reunification is appropriate or counterindicated. These provocative questions confront and challenge professionals working with families who abuse. Unfortunately, few criteria exist for making these difficult decisions, and no standardized instruments accurately measure parents' readiness to be safe and adequate parents.

When treatment is provided to families who abuse, treatment goals are developed while considering legal and welfare concerns. For example, if children are made dependents of the court, parents may be mandated to participate in therapy as a condition of reunification. Treatment plans therefore prioritize goals in terms of ensuring children's safety, reducing risk factors, and teaching safe and appropriate parenting. If parents cooperate with treatment and make progress, the court may deem them responsible for the care of their children. If parents are unwilling or unable to participate in treatment, and their dangerous behaviors remain unchanged, the court may retain custody of the children, and in extreme cases of parental noncompliance, may take action to terminate parental rights.

As this book has shown throughout, providing treatment services to abusive families is challenging. To further confound matters, a polarity of opinion, policy, and direction exists within social service, law enforcement, or judicial systems, which often overlap and other times seem mutually exclusive.

Historical Development of Reunification Efforts

The victim advocacy movement developed in connection with feminist ideology (Herman, 1981, 1992) and focused on all forms of violence against women and children, including physical abuse, sexual abuse and exploitation, domestic violence, and rape. In clinical practice, victim advocates emphasize the need to safeguard the rights and needs of children, seeking primarily to protect children's physical and emotional safety, even if this involves permanently separating abused children from their abusive parents. Child advocates believe that children should be free from the undue pressure of having to forgive and reconcile with formerly abusive parents, particularly in cases of incest.

The family preservation doctrine, by contrast, is based on the conviction that the biological family is the preferred childrearing unit and that most families can care for their children if properly assisted (Fritz, 1989; Maluccio, Waarsh, and Pine, 1993). Family preservationists seek to maintain the integrity of the family in almost all cases, on the assumption that increasing support and removing stressors can allow families to live together safely.

The conflict of priorities between victim advocacy and family preservation movements has made objective analysis of the issues involved extremely difficult. What little relevant research is available leaves professionals without empirically based guidelines for predicting risks and making reunification decisions. As a result of the intense feelings generated by the problem of child abuse by caretakers and of the scarcity of objective information to guide decisions, polarized opinions can emerge among professionals involved in the treatment of abusive families.

The Need for Specific Models

Under current legislation, policies exist that regulate state intervention in families in which children are physically or sexually abused or neglected by caretakers. This mandate is part of the Child Welfare and Adoption Assistance Act of 1980 (P.L. 96–272), which requires that states make reasonable efforts to prevent the institutionalization of children and to reunify separated families. This legislation requires the state to specify the problems that prompted removal and to design conditions that parents must meet if children are to be returned to their care. The state is also charged with the responsibility of assisting parents to accomplish these tasks (Pence, 1993). The law also mandates that judges presiding over child abuse cases determine whether child protective services workers have made reasonable efforts to protect children in the home before removing them.

The 1980 Child Welfare Act was written in response to a realization that the foster care system designed to protect children and provide temporary alternative care until families could be reunified was woefully flawed. Surveys of the welfare system by independent groups such as the Child Welfare League noted that children could not be guaranteed stability and safety within the foster care system. The Child Welfare League of America has conducted several studies on foster care. Their findings indicate that the average foster child moves five times, and that if children remain in foster care beyond eighteen months, it is likely they would stay in foster care "drift" until the age of majority. The Child Welfare Act proposed many reforms which have since been implemented, including periodic judicial and departmental reviews of children in care.

Despite the movement's stated goals and positive impact, several issues must be considered in connection with family preservation. For example, in cases of sexual abuse, the success rate in the treatment of sexual offenders is quite limited (Finkelhor, 1987; Pence, 1993). Also, there is no evidence to support the assumption that the benefits of family reunification outweigh the risks to child victims. In sexual abuse cases, recidivism often occurs many years subsequent to release from treatment (Finkelhor, 1987, p. 237). Few longitudinal studies have been done, however; thus, it is not currently known to what extent abuse recurs, and how abused children function in the long run (Pence, 1993). Follow-up studies are needed to provide critical information about decision-making procedures regarding reunification.

Special attention is warranted in child sexual abuse cases, given evidence that some incest offenders have well-entrenched sexual preferences for children and abuse them both in and out of the home (Abel and others, 1987). Reunification efforts may ensure that children in the home remain safe, but they may also give the false illusion that the problem has been adequately addressed. Although there are a number of research reports of successful treatment of individuals who sexually abuse, "some offenders are not amenable to treatment, and no reliable techniques exist for determining who these offenders are" (Finkelhor, 1987, p. 237). It is therefore imperative that treatment efforts be undertaken cautiously, with an eye toward children's ongoing safety.

Other problems have been identified in relation to family preservation legislation. The 1980 Child Welfare and Adoption Assistance Act fails to differentiate among various forms of child abuse, and fails to differentiate levels or categories of abuse within specific forms of child maltreatment.

Differences Among Forms of Child Abuse

Child maltreatment policies and interventions have been based on what Gelles (1992) calls the "tipping point" and "deficit" models of child maltreatment. The tipping point model is based on the idea that stresses and problems build up until a "tipping point" transforms a caring parent into an uncontrolled angry or aggressive parent. The deficit model assumes that some parents lack personal, social, or economic resources to be adequate parents, and that adding resources can help abusive parents become appropriate and competent parents. Obviously, these models are overshadowed by the need to prioritize children's safety, so that when children are in imminent danger of being reabused, support services are provided while children are safely cared for by substitute parents.

As illustrated earlier in this book, typical interventions for abusive parents include support, guidance and education, and efforts to help parents identify, address, and cope more effectively with internal and external stressors. Parent aid and respite-care programs, early interventions such as those provided by Healthy Start programs that begin after childbirth, self-help, Homebuilders, or more formal counseling, and parenting training can also be helpful in reducing some forms of child abuse, including neglect. And yet, in order to be effective, another dimension of services must be provided.

Successful interventions in severe cases of physical abuse and neglect and intrafamilial sexual abuse typically include a period of separation between abused children and abusive parents, specialized evaluation and treatment of abused children, specialized evaluation and treatment of abusive and nonabusive parents, and visitation and reunification strategies that are contingent upon thorough assessment of family members' functioning and progress towards specified goals (O'Connell, 1986; Orenchuk-Tomiuk, Matthey, and Pigler Christensen, 1990; Orten and Rich, 1988; Roizner-Hayes, 1994; Smith, 1994; Trepper and Barrett, 1989).

A common problem of family preservation initiatives has been their tendency to simply extrapolate interventions used in the treatment of physical abuse and neglect to the treatment of incest. This "one size fits all intervention" (Gelles, 1994) often puts children at serious risk. A more effective approach is for clinicians to become familiar with treatment programs and models that demonstrate successful interventions, such as Meinig and Bonner's (1990) treatment approach for working with incest families.

Differences Within Specific Types of Abuse

Regardless of the nature or severity of the abuse, current child protective policies assume that preserving families (preventing separation, or if separation occurs, reuniting families as early as possible) is the preferred goal. The literature indicates, however, that there are different categories of abuse and abusers (Chaffin, 1994; Finkelhor, 1984; Wolfner and Gelles, 1993), and that interventions must vary according to the nature and severity of the offense. Roizner-Hayes (1994) studied professional responses to reunification and found that most respondents believed that reunification should not be an option in cases of severe abuse.

The notion that subcategories of abuse exist was introduced by Wolfner and Gelles (1993), whose national study on violence against children showed that parents who cause severe or lethal harm to their children are categorically different from parents whose maltreatment does not involve life-threatening harm to children. Different categories of offenders exist in terms of incestuous abuse as well (Chaffin, 1994; Finkelhor, 1984). Some molest in response to stress or opportunity; others are compulsive predators of children. Some individuals entice children through special treatment and rewards; others use fear, force, and threats.

Why Is Separation Necessary?

Many professionals question the need for separation of family members after identification of abuse. Although it is easier to "see" the damage inflicted by physical abuse or neglect, in cases of incest, opinions about what needs to happen (especially in regard to the child's placement outside the home) differ greatly. Some professionals argue that although victims want the abuse to stop, they do not necessarily want their abusers to be removed from the home and that financial burden on family resources results from forced separation (Giarretto, 1982).

It is interesting to note that these arguments are not salient when children have been beaten. Physically abused children likewise want the beatings to stop, but they do not want their parents to be punished, and often, because of maladaptive role reversals, abused children worry incessantly about their abusive parents if they are separated from them.

Separation is a safety measure to protect children from both overt abuse (actual incidents) and covert abuse (emotional abuse dynamics). Preferably, abused children should be allowed to stay home and abusive parents should be the ones to leave (Berliner, 1986; Herman, 1981; Meinig and Bonner, 1990; O'Connell, 1986), especially when there is one functional, protective, and appropriate caretaker. Children are too often removed, however, when abusers refuse or cannot be trusted to leave the home, or when nonabusive parents are not willing or able to ensure their children's safety. Asking parents who abuse to leave the home is more fair than disrupting children's lives by placing them in unfamiliar environments, an act that is often thought of as benign, but which can feel traumatic to already-injured children. Asking (or mandating) that abusers leave the home places responsibility on the adult who abuses, and reinforces negative consequences for the abusive behavior. Removal from the home can provide people who abuse with incentives to change, if changes are stipulated as conditions for their return home (Berliner, 1986). Separation is also necessary to create adequate conditions for the evaluation and treatment of different family members.

In assessing the incestuous parent, it is important to determine "the full extent of the deviancy, the potential for predation, and the degree of compulsiveness of the offending behavior" (O'Connell, 1986, p. 376). In assessing the state of the child who has been victimized, clinical experience suggests that it may be contraindicated to encourage children to disclose possible sexual abuse if they have to go home with the parent who allegedly abused them. When sexual abuse evaluations are conducted while the child is living in the home with the alleged incest offender, the potential for false negatives or for recantation may increase.

Professionals working with abusive families have learned that leaving children in contact with abusive parents is inappropriate for a number of reasons. Even after the abuse is disclosed and treatment is provided to the abuser, access to children creates a high risk of reabuse. In sexual abuse, arousal patterns are not easily changed or controlled; in physical violence, impulsivity and rage are difficult to reduce; in cases of neglect, teaching parents appropriate parental instincts is difficult at best, since many neglectful parents are incapacitated in some way (by drugs, physical or mental problems, general underfunctioning, or extreme immaturity). Allowing abusers to remain in the home places an excessive burden on victimized children, on other children in the home, and on nonabusive parents, who may feel like unwilling or ineffectual watchdogs.

Moreover, when abusers remain in the home, there is not enough emphasis on the fact that the abuser is 100 percent responsible for the abusive actions. Under these circumstances, abused children may feel that nothing really happened as a result of their (risky) disclosure, that the offense was not important, or that they are to blame or deserved the abuse.

Lastly, separation can be used as a way for professionals to have leverage to encourage change in the abuser and the family system. Visitation and family reunification can become incentives for family members to participate in treatment to change the dynamics that contributed to the abuse.

Making Recommendations Regarding Reunification

Reunification is a process of progressively increased contact between abused children, abusers, and other family members that evolves from planned, short, supervised meetings toward the least restrictive living arrangement that ensures physical and emotional security for all children in the family. Pre-reunification stages serve two purposes: they allow family members to reestablish contact under the safest possible conditions, and they serve a diagnostic purpose, allowing parent-child interactions to be observed and evaluated by trained professionals.

The reconstitution of abusive families requires professionals to determine the risk of continued physical and emotional abuse. Premature reunification may force children to live in a state of hypervigilance and anxiety, hindering their ability to recover from the impact of abuse. When children are returned to incestuous families without sufficient changes in family attitudes, behaviors, and interactions, they may feel pressure to pretend the abuse never happened, or they may feel unable to prevent reoccurrence of abuse dynamics. Feelings of guilt, shame, and responsibility, commonly found in abused children, may be exacerbated if family reunification occurs and the child is directly or indirectly blamed for the abuse or family disruption. Abused children may feel unsupported, invalidated, anxious, and disempowered without their family's nurturing and encouragement.

Determining Readiness of the Nonabusive Parent

The nonabusive parent's reaction to the identification of child abuse is key to the family's future. The nonabusive parent must decide whether to maintain a relationship with the abuser, or to separate from him or her temporarily or permanently. In some cases, the nonabusive parent wants to work towards rebuilding his or her marriage or relationship. If this goal is realistic and the parent's desire to reconstitute the relationship does not override the best interests of the child, reunification can be viewed as a treatment goal.

The fate of abused children is highly dependent on the nonabusive parent's ability and willingness to keep the children out of harm's way, and to provide definitive protective action when warranted. One vivid example of a family in which reunification was a stated but unrealistic goal was a case of chronic domestic violence, in which the wife had been repeatedly beaten, treated by physicians who encouraged her to leave the home, seduced into believing that the abuse would stop, and beaten again and again. This mother had often said to herself that if her husband ever hit her child she would not hesitate to leave. The first and second time, she did go to a shelter, and protective services was pleased with her resolve to get a job and prepare for a permanent separation; but the mother was not able to keep herself from allowing her husband into the home, although out of concern for her child, she would only allow him in during the night. Eventually, as she again became convinced that he had changed, she allowed him to spend more and more time in the house, while reassuring protective services and her therapist that she was no longer seeing him.

The child's play therapist became concerned about the child when she began displaying anxious and aggressive behavior after a period of stabilization. Eventually the child confided that there were monsters in the house at night who yelled and screamed. It did not take long for the child to reveal it was her father, who was visiting the mother at night and causing the child great concern.

In spite of the fact that the mother both loved her spouse and wanted to help him and was earnestly concerned for her child's welfare, reunification in this case was not sensible or safe. The father's drug habit, coupled with his unwillingness to seek or maintain recovery, created a very unsafe situation for mother and child. Eventually the child was placed in foster care, and it was this action that allowed the mother to confront the reality of her situation. Torn by the pain of separation from her daughter, the mother was able to focus on making changes that would allow them to reunite.

Determining the Abused Child's Readiness

Abused children must also become willing and able to report inappropriate or problematic behavior. Reunification readiness requires an extraordinary amount of work focused on children's self-protection, including clear and realistic safety plans, access to people who can help, and an ability (as mentioned in Chapter Four) to identify and describe warning signs. Sometimes children develop an exaggerated sense of power and imagine that they will handle future abuse in an unrealistic way. Consider the following example in which a sexually abused boy of eight talks about prevention with Dr. E. Gil:

THERAPIST: So, you don't think your dad will touch you in your privates again.

CHILD: Nope. He said he wouldn't do that. He won't.

THERAPIST: So you think he won't because he said so.

CHILD: Uh-hum.

THERAPIST: Do you remember when he promised to stop before?

CHILD: Uh-hum.

THERAPIST: Tell me about that.

CHILD: That was when it was a secret.

THERAPIST: And what happened?

CHILD: [*Whispers in therapist's ear*] He promised he wouldn't do it again, and then he did.

THERAPIST: What did you think about that?

CHILD: He lied.

THERAPIST: And how did you feel?

CHILD: Sad.

THERAPIST: Sad?

CHILD: Uh-hum.

THERAPIST: What other feelings?

CHILD: [*Whispers in therapist's ear again*] Sort of mad.

THERAPIST: Sort of mad. That makes sense. Your dad broke his promise and you were sad and sort of mad.

CHILD: Yup.

THERAPIST: What do you think you might do if your dad breaks his promise again?

CHILD: He won't now. It's not secret no more.

THERAPIST: Oh, so other people know about it now. It's not a secret anymore.

CHILD: That's right.

THERAPIST: I see. So, I wonder what would happen if he broke his promise again, even though it's not a secret now.

CHILD: Mom says I should bite him down there.

THERAPIST: Your mom says you should bite him. Hum. I'm not sure about that. What do you think?

CHILD: That would hurt daddy.

THERAPIST: What do you think you could do?

CHILD: I could kick him.

THERAPIST: Okay, so that's two things you can do to fight back. What else do you think you could do?

CHILD: Yell.

THERAPIST: Uh-hum. You could yell. What would you say?

CHILD: Daddy stop. You promised no more.

THERAPIST: So you'd remind your dad he made a promise.

CHILD: Yup.

THERAPIST: And what else?

CHILD: I'm tired now. Can't think anymore about it.

THERAPIST: Okay, well you did some good work. Talked about how to keep yourself safe. We'll talk to mom and dad about this some more so maybe they have some more ideas, too.

CHILD: Okay, can we draw now?

In order for clinicians to feel confident that the formerly abused child has integrated ideas about what he or she might do or say if abuse were to surface anew, they might have to persist and address the topic over a few sessions, bringing in parents to add important information. Because all forms of abuse tend to surface in the context of secrecy and denial, these open conversations create a healthy atmosphere that will positively impact family interactions.

Reunification is contraindicated if children continue to exhibit abuse-related symptoms or lack of emotional stability. For reunification to be undertaken, children should feel comfortable in the presence of the abusive parent. Signs of extreme or chronic discomfort or apprehension must be carefully evaluated by clinicians and parents alike. At the same time, it is unrealistic to expect that children who have been separated from their parents will feel fully content immediately. There may be some initial awkwardness or even acting-out behavior, in which case it is crucial to observe parental abilities to be aware of, sensitive, and responsive to their children's behaviors. If parents perceive their children's discomfort or apprehension as a sign of rejection that provokes their anger or resentment, these are poor prognostic signs of improved parental functioning. Conversely, parents who are empathetic and make efforts to decrease their children's anxiety are demonstrating positive parenting, particularly if the changes are motivated by internal shifts, as opposed to efforts to impress the evaluators.

Finally, although we have mentioned the importance of considering the child's wishes, relying on them exclusively is problematic. Abused children seem to have particularly intense loyalty to their abusive parents, perhaps because they long for their love and approval. Professionals must consider children's statements in relation to other factors, such as the level and type of attachment (secure or insecure), their reactions to separation and visitation, and the availability of a nurturing alternative living arrangement (such as relatives or adoption).

Visitation

Visitation is an essential component of reunification assessment and planning. Like all important decisions involving more than an individual family member, it is important that decisions regarding visitation be part of a coordinated plan among all professionals involved. Changes in the structure of visitation, risk assessment, and the review of visits should not be done without the input of all parties who are in a position to observe family interactions and provide relevant information. Too often, the courts, protective services workers, or therapists make recommendations and decisions without consulting parties who may have access to information indicating problems, risks, or conversely, positive experiences in relation to visitation.

Visitation decisions in cases of child abuse must be fully explored. It is often advisable that visitation between abused children and abusive parents be suspended while an evaluation is undertaken. Even if visits are supervised, contact with the alleged abuser during an evaluation period can significantly increase the chances of evaluations in which no disclosure is made or in which disclosures are followed by swift recantations.

A range of options exist regarding visits between parents who abuse and their children. Visitation may be supervised by a family member or by a professional, and may take place in a number of different settings (such as a child protective services office, a therapists' office, a visitation center, or a relative's home) according to what is clinically indicated. Visits should be suspended if there are indications that they are having a negative impact on the child's mental status, if the child resists the visits, if the parent fails to follow visitation rules (for example, talking about sensitive topics, or making inappropriate physical contact), or if there is any indication of intimidation.

Supervisors overseeing visitations must be well trained to conduct visits, and must know specifically what constitutes desirable and undesirable parent-child interactions. In the course of our work, we have encountered supervisors who seemed oblivious to their responsibilities and who had limited understanding of their roles and responsibilities, thereby allowing abusers opportunities to sequester children, talk to them out of ear shot, or engage in suggestive or coercive physical contact.

In contrast, there are trained supervisors who know full well that they have a significant task, who monitor verbal and nonverbal communications as well as positive or negative interactions between parents and children. Trained supervisors are ready to step in at a moment's notice, and feel confident to set limits on inappropriate or suggestive behavior when needed.

Chapter Four discussed the need to use direct observation of the parent-child relationship as a diagnostic measure as well as to gauge therapeutic progress. In preparation for reunification, it is essential to observe abused children with their formerly abusive parents. During these therapeutic observations, clinicians observe and document the child's affect and behavior (for example, does the child exhibit sexualized behavior?), as well as parental responses to the child. If the child is defiant, uncomfortable, anxious, or sexualized, what does the parent say or do in response, and are parental responses appropriate, inappropriate, or indicative of problem areas?

I (Gil) was conducting supervised visits, observing through a one-way mirror. Although both the social worker and I had recommended no contact for an extended period of time, the court had required supervised visitations under my watchful eye. Suddenly, the four-year-old boy reached out and grabbed the father's crotch, and the father giggled and grabbed the child's crotch. This interaction was fleeting, and I bolted into the therapy room, took the child's hand and talked to both of them about how it was not okay for them to touch each others' crotches. The father responded that they were "playing," and in my individual session with him later I pointed out to him that this type of game is exactly what precipitated his more explicit sexual "games" with his child. The father's inability to respond to the child by setting limits, and his minimizing my intervention, appearing surprised that I would think the grabbing behavior unusual, were red flags that indicated the father's limited progress.

This exact situation came up with another parent who was with his child in a supervised visit. In striking contrast, when the child grabbed the father's crotch, this father grabbed the child's hands in his, told him calmly and seriously that it was not okay for him to touch daddy in his privates, adding that daddy would not touch him in his privates either. In this case, the father interpreted the child's touching as a way the child was asking for limits and reassurance that dad would not touch his genitals again. The father's response was very appropriate and when I talked with him later individually, he said that he had rehearsed with his therapist how he would respond if his child did any inappropriate touching.

Reunification Programs: Stages and Structure

The risks posed by the reestablishment of the relationship between abused child and abusive parent cannot be emphasized enough (Meinig and Bonner, 1990). A number of programs have developed guidelines for reunification to reduce the risks of revictimization (Giarretto, 1982; Meinig and Bonner, 1990; O'Connell, 1986; Server and Janzen, 1982; Trepper and Barrett, 1989). Typically, these programs are fairly well structured, delineating treatment stages and conditions that allow a family to proceed toward reunification. O'Connell (1986) for instance, specifies goals and conditions for the following treatment stages:

1. Reestablishment of contact (including apology letters to the victim) (p. 377)

2. First visits (supervision of contact and identification of a reliable supervisor) (p. 379)

3. Family outings (supervised visits outside the home so that home can remain a "safe refuge" for the child) (p. 381)

4. Visits home (parents must respect children's boundaries, never entering their bedrooms or bathrooms without permission, and must remain fully dressed) (p. 382)

5. Overnight visits (use of locks on bedroom doors, particularly in incest cases; parents must remain in their room at night) (p. 384)

Similarly, Meinig and Bonner (1990) have designed a treatment program for incest fathers that includes five phases: specialized treatment services, including individual, marital, group, and family therapy for all family members; visitation outside the home; in-home visitation; overnight visitation; and completion of reunification process.

Trepper and Barrett (1989), who also designed a treatment program for incestuous families, set forth the following conditions for reunification:

1. The child indicates that he or she feels safe.

2. A safety plan has been developed with the child.

3. The therapist has verified the safety plan.

4. The family can identify, acknowledge, and understand risk factors.

5. Precipitating factors have been corrected.

6. All family members acknowledge the facts of the abuse.

7. There is recognition and acknowledgment of responsibility and impact.

8. The nonabusive parent is willing and capable of protecting the children.

9. No secrecy exists in regard to the abuse. Significant members of the extended family are aware of the abuse.

These authors primarily address the issue of reunification of incestuous families, yet these conditions or goals in treatment would also be helpful in reunification efforts with other types of abuse. Professionals agree that therapy identifies, acknowledges, and addresses family dynamics that may have contributed to abuse. In addition, the nonabusive parent must take a position of authority as well as a protective stance, to ensure that he or she neither places the child in harm's way nor fails to respond to dangerous situations.

Professionals also redirect traditionally closed family systems to access outside support and contact. Increased involvement with outsiders breaks the isolation that so often contributes to dysfunctional family dynamics (Fish and Faynik, 1989). The family structure that existed prior to the abuse must be reorganized. Meinig and Bonner (1990) go so far as to transfer all decision-making power regarding the children to the nonabusive parent; the formerly abusive parent can make suggestions, but final decisions rest with the nonabusive parent. In Gil's experience, some nonabusive parents are capable of this type of responsibility; other parents may feel overloaded and unwilling to be in a relationship that imposes rigid guidelines. The critical factor is for family structure to be discussed with family members, making sure that circumstances that led to the abusive use of power do not surface anew.

In order to feel optimistic (and safe) about the family's chances of safe reintegration, most therapists and agency personnel interested in reunification impose conditions on each family member and expect to see considerable gains.

Checklist for Reunification of Incestuous Families

The Checklist for Reunification of Incestuous Families (CRIF) is a tool developed to assess child and parental factors relevant to reunification. The tool is based on data obtained from a 1994 study by Roizner-Hayes of 105 highly experienced therapists who were asked to give their professional opinions about the reconstitution of families with histories of father-child incest. The study surveyed professional attitudes as well as criteria used to make decisions or recommendations regarding reunification. Subjects ranked child and parental factors in terms of their relevance for assessing incestuous families' readiness for reunification.

The importance of having clear criteria on which to base recommendations cannot be overstated, as it diminishes professional tendencies to espouse philosophical agendas in particular cases. The CRIF can assist professionals involved in the treatment of abusive families in a number of ways:

- Evaluation of child and parental factors relevant to the decision to reunify
- Identification of risks/contraindications to reunification
- Identification of child and parental strengths
- Identification of areas of agreement and disagreement among professionals
- Coordination of interventions among professionals
- Determination of treatment goals at different stages of treatment

When used as a tool to obtain and coordinate information from different sources, the CRIF can facilitate group decision making by maximizing access to information and providing a "reality check" to countertransferential responses that may be experienced by professionals. The CRIF encourages communication and forces professionals to stay close to the data when making decisions. Regardless of professional views about preserving families, advocating for children, or both, the CRIF allows the discussion to remain focused.

Although this instrument was developed for making determinations in incest cases, the issues of safety, protection, and best interests of the child apply to other forms of abuse as well. The following criteria will aid the process of decision making and rendering clinical recommendations regarding reunification in all cases of abuse:

Factors Relevant to Individuals Who Abuse

Acknowledgment or denial of the facts of the abuse

Understanding or denial of the effects of the abuse on the child

Ability to put the child's interests and needs above one's own

Willingness to continue in treatment after reunification

Adherence to treatment recommendations

Empathy for the child

Progress toward behavioral goals

Appropriateness of behavior toward the child during scheduled visits

Degree of remorse, or lack of it

Compliance with rules during visitation

Participation in recommended services

Emotional functioning

Specific issues addressed in treatment

Willingness to offer apologies and amends to child

History of past or current use of drugs including alcohol

History of domestic violence

Acknowledgment and involvement in treatment for other problems

Progress toward psychodynamic goals

Nature of interpersonal relationships and supports

Willingness to plead guilty in court

Therapist's view about readiness to reunify

Attendance to scheduled visits with child

Perception of current relationship with spouse/partner

Parenting skills

Cognitive functioning

Length of time in treatment

Type of therapy undertaken

Past and current work status

Factors Related to Nonabusive Parents

Ability to protect child

Ability to confront abuser and report inappropriate behavior

Acknowledgment or denial of the facts of the abuse

Acknowledgment or denial of the effects of the abuse

Adherence to treatment recommendations

Compliance and enforcement of recommended rules

Ability to put the child's interests and needs above one's own

Empathy for the child

Ability to protect self

Appropriateness of behavior toward child

Participation in recommended services

Past and current history of drug and alcohol abuse

Emotional functioning

Progress toward behavioral goals

Past or current victimization by domestic violence

Attendance to scheduled visits and appointments

Perception of relationship with spouse or partner

Parenting skills

Participation in recommended services

Nature of interpersonal relationships and supports

Actions (protective/nonprotective) upon learning about abuse

Progress toward psychodynamic goals

Therapist's view about family reunification

Specific issues addressed in treatment

Cognitive functioning

Type of therapy undertaken

Length of time in treatment

Past and current work history

Factors Related to Abused Children

Willingness and ability to report inappropriate behavior by abuser

Available supports within family

Current emotional functioning

Perception of nonabusive parent's ability to protect

Perception of nonabusive parent's view of the abuse

Comfort and safety in presence of abuser

Perceptions of abuser's view of the abuse

Progress toward therapy goals

Available supports outside the family to whom unacceptable parental behavior can be reported

Perception of nonabusive parent's ability to meet needs

Behavior after visits with abuser

Perception of abuser's ability to meet needs

Behavior toward abuser

Behavior after visits with nonabusive parent

Behavior toward nonabusive parent

Specific issues that have been addressed in child's therapy

Behavior prior to visits with abuser

Therapist's Views About the Appropriateness of Child and Family Reunification

Developmental considerations

Behavior prior to visits with nonabusive parents

Reactions to being taken away from family

Cognitive functioning

Wishes about reunification

Attachment to abuser

Emotional functioning at time the abuse was disclosed

Type of therapy received by child

Length of time in therapy

Length of time in foster care

Attachment to foster care providers

Foster parents' observations of child after visits

The process of family reunification is long, complex, and time consuming for all involved. Many families lack the strength, commitment, endurance, and resources to successfully overcome the problems that contribute to child abuse and to meet all the conditions required by reunification. The potential risks involved in reunifying abused children with formerly abusive parents require extreme caution among professionals who are making decisions regarding reunification.

Structured programs based on clearly stipulated stages, conditions, and rules in relation to visitation and reunification are the treatment of choice for abusive families who wish to reunify. The CRIF (see Appendix for complete tool) offers organized criteria that can facilitate coordination of treatment and evaluation of families over time. The assessment of strengths, risks, progress, difficulties, and problems is essential to maintaining focused attention on the child's best interest.

6

Treatment Failures

One of the most useful books I have read was entitled *Failures in Family Therapy* (Coleman, 1985). It convinced me of what I knew instinctively: each mistake, although painful at the time, teaches us important lessons that shape our professional development.

As an author, I have noticed a previously unconscious leaning toward committing my successes to the printed word, yet when I lecture, I find it liberating to converse freely about the many lessons I have experienced over the years. This chapter is my first attempt to write down some of the lessons I have learned through trial and error.

Setting Children Up to Fail

During an internship program in Oakland, California, I worked with a ten-year-old physically abused African-American child, who, due to the fact that he was one of my first clients, received my undivided attention and endured all my eager attempts to be helpful.

A policy existed in this internship program that clinicians either worked with children *or* with their parents, but seldom did clinicians conduct family therapy sessions, although child and adult therapists discussed treatment goals and strategies on occasion.

My child client, Antony, was a very angry child. He had been chronically physically abused by both parents, and he was under his mother's care. His mother had made a commitment to stop hitting him and had met all conditions of the court in order to keep her child at home with her.

Antony was an aggressive child who was diagnosed with conduct disorder. One of my first goals was to help him deal with his anger in more constructive ways. I worked with Antony every week on finding new ways to express his anger. I initiated several strategies, none very effective. He liked the notion of tearing up telephone books, but he tired of that eventually. Besides, he did not have telephone books at home. He insisted on punching a BOBO (an inflatable punching bag for children), and did so gleefully. I noticed, however, that every time he had a session with the BOBO, he subsequently got into a physical altercation at school. It appeared that this release of physical energy in some way facilitated or reinforced his physical violence.

When he hit the BOBO, I tried to get him to verbalize his anger: "Put words to that fist," I would holler, "What are you saying to BOBO?" Antony would say, "Fuck you asshole," and become more and more agitated. I finally removed the BOBO from the playroom. Antony needed help containing his angry emotions, not emoting.

He liked molding clay, and often he would stab the clay with the sculpting instruments I provided. Because of my limited experience, and the fact that he seemed to become more physical after these meetings as well, the clay work was also short-lived.

I had him draw people he was mad at, and I encouraged him to write over the pictures everything he wanted to say to them. He instinctively wrote four-letter words and then he crumpled up the papers and used them to shoot baskets. He liked disposing of those pictures, perhaps symbolically destroying the people he did not like. This exercise was moderately successful.

Finally, I worked with him with a tape recorder. He loved the concept of talking as loud as he could and then hearing himself. I took this opportunity to have him role play with me what he could say when he was angry at somebody. The first few attempts he shouted obscenities. Then I started saying, "I don't know what those words mean, tell me what you really mean," or "Talk to me in other words," and finally he began yelling that he was mad because I (in role) hurt his feelings, or that he was mad because I (in role) did not understand. I started repeating back what I heard him say, and it calmed him down quite a bit when I was reflective with him. "You are angry because I hurt your feelings. I'm sorry, I didn't mean to hurt your feelings."

Antony concentrated intensely when he listened to the tape recording of our conversations, and eventually he took some of them home. I told him that he was getting so good at saying what was really bothering him that he should try it out when he felt angry. He chose to experiment at home.

I could not get him to tell me much about what was going on at home with his experiments but he seemed dejected and less emotionally available than he was before. One day he appeared with redness in his eye and said he had walked into a door (an excuse he had used once before when his mother punched him in the face).

To make a very long story short, I told my supervisor about this injury, a child abuse report was filed, and I came to find out, painfully, that every time Antony told his mother how he felt, she slapped him across the face. I had inadvertently set this child up to fail by teaching him something that provoked his mother's wrath.

This taught me about the necessity of making and maintaining contact with family members when I am working with children, and checking out the desirability of the lessons I am teaching them. In retrospect, I would have liked to talk to the mother, to have found out how she handled his anger and what she would have encouraged me to teach her son about expressing anger in a safe way. My failure to inquire, and my lax attitude about pursuing meetings with Antony's mothers' therapist, put the child at risk of being reabused—a sobering lesson.

I now discuss a child's problem behaviors with his or her parents, and I ask them in what ways this behavior is a problem to them and what actions they have tried to help the child stop the behavior, and then we decide together what interventions might be effective so that what I teach children in therapy is acceptable to their parents and is therefore reinforced at home.

Wanting to Know Too Much Too Soon

This example concerns a forty-one-year-old Colombian man, Mr. Diaz, referred to me by a colleague primarily because I am Spanish-speaking and had some experience working with individuals who molest children. My colleague was treating Mr. Diaz's twelve-year-old sexually abused daughter. Mr. Diaz was currently living with his cousins. He plea bargained (admitting culpability) to avoid a prison sentence, accepting probation and mandated treatment. Mrs. Diaz had been shocked to learn about the incest, but had reconciled herself to forgiving her husband and taking him back as long as he got the help he needed. She had initially been very angry at her daughter for not telling her about the year-long sexual abuse, but eventually she realized that her daughter was bound to secrecy by a father who pleaded with her not to destroy the family and kept promising that each incident of sexual abuse would be the last.

In our first appointment, Mr. Diaz was compliant and shy, barely making eye contact with me. He had never been in therapy and readily admitted that the whole idea was alien. I asked him what he expected therapy would be like, and he could not come up with a response. When I explained that this was verbal therapy and that we would talk about his perceptions, thoughts, and feelings, in particular regarding the incest, he squirmed in his seat.

I could not judge whether he was in acute denial or just painfully timid, so I forged ahead and asked him to tell me what he could about the sexual abuse. I told him I knew he had pleaded guilty, and that I wanted to understand the nature and extent of the abuse with his daughter.

He responded by telling me that his lawyers had told him to

plea bargain to avoid going to jail. I then asked if he was saying he had not committed the sexual offenses for which he was charged. He said, "No, I didn't say that." Trying to get a straight answer out of him was excruciating.

Finally I said, "Your daughter has told her teacher and therapist that you fondled her and put your fingers inside her vagina, is this true?" My tone was matter-of-fact, and I tried to communicate that it would be safe for him to talk about what he had done, and that talking about what happened would be part of the treatment.

He looked away, with tears welling up and he stated solemnly, "My daughter does not lie."

I then proceeded to ask him if he had touched her on top of or underneath her clothes. He was noncommittal. I asked if he had touched her during the day, or the night. He said he went into her room at night. I asked what part of the body he fondled and he said he was not really sure.

Since he had arrived late to our first meeting, we barely got through these questions by the time the session came to an end. We made an appointment for the following week and he left.

His probation officer called me the next day. I was not surprised to hear that Mr. Diaz wanted a different therapist, but I was surprised to hear why. He felt that I was too young, and he did not understand how someone so young could know anything about sexual matters in men. The probation officer was reluctant to refer Mr. Diaz to someone else since the officer and I had worked together on other cases, he trusted me, and he was quite sure that this problem could be worked through.

I thought about the first session with Mr. Diaz a great deal and eventually realized that I had overlooked certain important issues. First, I am a Latin woman. In Latin America, women professionals are scarce, and I did not take the time to provide him with my credentials so he would understand that I was trained in the area of mental health, and child sexual abuse in particular.

In addition, in Latin America sexuality is a subject that men and women do not discuss together. Whether men discuss sex with other men is a mystery to me, and women are only recently exploring this issue more openly. Consequently, for Mr. Diaz, not only was the concept of therapy unfamiliar, but the idea of talking about sex with a woman was outlandish.

On further reflection, my view of the meeting with Mr. Diaz was that I had probably also been too intimidating to him by focusing on the issue of sexuality without waiting for a "reasonable period of time" before introducing this private and potentially threatening topic. My training in working with sexual offenders told me to gauge how much denial exists immediately and to set a matter-of-fact tone about sexual abuse. In this way it is clear from the very first (intake) session that the treatment will focus on stopping sexual abuse by addressing precipitants (thoughts, affects, and behaviors).

After careful consideration, I approached the second session differently and took two specific actions to remedy his ambivalence about my capacity to be of help: I wore a white lab coat with a name tag that said Dr. Eliana Gil, and I brought a copy of my résumé so we could review my credentials and he could see that I had been well trained in working in the area of sexual abuse. I also decided to slow down the questions about sexuality, and instead took a complete history of his childhood, adolescence, and all other events leading up to his current situation.

This history-taking phase lasted about four sessions, and as I gleaned personal information, the therapeutic relationship began to develop. To further strengthen the therapeutic alliance, I often asked him how to say particular words in Spanish, which gave him a certain feeling that he knew more than I did about the language and that he could be of help to me.

After I compiled his social history, I reviewed the facts with him, asking for sexual information, which he had not volunteered. By asking about his sexuality as a child, and by telling him whenever I could that his sexual interests at that time were normative (if they were), we slowly desensitized the subject so it was much easier for him to talk about the details of the sexual abuse, which he needed to provide in order for me to talk about cognitive restructuring, arousal patterns, relapse prevention, and other topics necessary to discuss when in working with men who sexually abuse children.

To summarize, in my first session with Mr. Diaz, I was insensitive to cultural issues that I understand full well, by both failing to establish myself as a professional and by rushing the subject of sexuality, which is not openly discussed in Latin cultures. In retrospect, my own discomfort with discussing sexuality with a Latin man (breaking some of the rules I grew up with) provoked anxiety which I handled by asking too much too soon, and by trying to get the uncomfortable subject of sexuality quickly out of the way.

False Illusion of Safety

I have been working with prevention and treatment of child abuse since 1973. Early on, I worked as a sponsor with Parents Anonymous (a self-help group for parents who physically abuse their children), was a telephone crisis counselor for parents under stress (the TALK Line in San Francisco), and ran drop-in groups for single parents and parents wanting to discuss parenting issues. In the course of this work I met many violent individuals whose primary interactions were hostile and defiant.

I especially remember that during my years with Parents Anonymous some of the parents who were beating their children were also beating each other and that such domestic violence was not an unusual occurrence. Likewise, it was not unusual to work with parents who abused their children in a variety of ways, not just one.

Somewhere along the line I learned to set clear limits on confrontations and violence in a calm and direct manner. I got pretty good at doing this, and I developed a false sense of security, or invulnerability, that I have discussed with other colleagues working in the field of abuse. I think this sense of invulnerability originates from a feeling that in order to be effective you have to remain in control, and you cannot let yourself feel intimidated or frightened because it decreases your effectiveness (you give away your power).

So I got very good at looking at very large, very hostile people (usually men) and saying calmly, "I will not accept your hitting or hurting me in any way," instructing them to sit down, talk to me in a lower pitch, or come back when they felt better able to verbalize their concerns in a more appropriate manner. No one ever hit me or hurt me, and although I felt intimidated and frightened some of the time, I learned to behave in a way that I believed kept me safe.

I have since come to realize that it is better to acknowledge feelings of fear, and not to feel too confident that everyone will accept limits equally well.

The case example I will describe now occurred a number of years ago, and sometimes in workshops I talk about it, ostensibly because I like to share what I learned from the experience, but more to the point, because each time I talk about it I process the experience a little bit more.

I was asked to conduct a court-mandated evaluation in a case in which a four-year-old Caucasian child named Lily had alleged that her father had "hurt" her privates. The parents had separated due to the father's violent outbursts, marital infidelities, and drinking. Although the family court allowed regular visitation after the legal separation, the mother noted that Lily wanted to stay home and refused to visit her father. When the mother asked why Lily did not want to visit her father, she volunteered that he had hurt her vagina. Mother immediately called her attorney and filed a motion to suspend his visitation rights. Family court heard the case and ordered the evaluation, suspending all visitation until my report was completed.

I conducted the evaluation in standard form. I met with the mother and father separately for two hours each. I took a psychosocial history and listened to each of them discuss their perceptions of what the child had said, why she suddenly did not feel comfortable visiting dad, and if it was possible that anyone else might have hurt the child's genitals. I also asked both parents to described their child's personality, likes and dislikes, hobbies, preferred food, TV shows, books, and so forth.

The mother seemed to know multiple details about her daughter, and readily offered information about the child's disposition, temperament, schedule, preferred activities, and so on. The father was strikingly unable to say much about the child except how pretty she was and how she looked exactly like a smaller version of his wife. He mentioned the fact that the child looked like his wife at least four times, and although this was true, it seemed odd to have him point that out repeatedly. He also called the child by his wife's name once during our interview, which in and of itself is not unusual, but which, in the context of his almost obsessive focus on his wife, became more relevant.

He was brief in all his responses, and seemed to jump ahead quickly to describing his courtship with his wife, their wedding, their honeymoon, and the circumstances that led to their current situation. Rather than mentioning the fact that he had hit his wife on two occasions, that he had routine physical altercations in neighborhood bars, that he drank too much, and that he had a volatile temper, he explained that his wife's parents were the problem, that they always interfered, that they took her in instead of sending her back home where she belonged, and that they exaggerated the normal squabbles he and his wife had. When I pointed out that I had seen police reports of domestic violence calls, he again quickly stated that the police did not listen to his side of the story and that it "wasn't as bad as it looked."

I then met with Lily for at least nine visits. I used play therapy techniques to facilitate symbolic communication about her perceptions, thoughts, and concerns. She provided vast information about the fights at home, how her mommy had cuts and blood on her face, how her daddy was mean to mommy, but he was not mean to her (a fact verified by mother). Finally we talked about what it was like to be at daddy's house and she said it was "fine in the daytime." After she explained that in the daytime she watched TV, ate lunch, and played outside, she said, "At night daddy hurts me." When I asked her to show me (with dolls) how daddy hurt her, she put the child doll in the bed, had the dad doll come into the room, take the covers off and touch the doll between the legs.

It was interesting to note that during this play the child became very anxious, moving in a rigid manner and whispering. She care-fully removed the doll's underwear, attempted to open her legs (the doll would not cooperate), and said, "Daddy sticks his finger in my privates." When I asked her which private the finger goes inside, she said, "Where I pee." When she demonstrated this activity, she looked at the little doll and she said, "She's sad," and added, "I don't like daddy to do that."

Her statements remained consistent and she volunteered them throughout our meetings, often saying she did not want to go to daddy's house alone or at night. This was an interesting statement from a child who obviously loved and missed her dad, and was will-ing to see him during the day when it was safe, and when someone else was there, but did not want to feel unsafe when she was alone with him.

My mistake was a grave one: I had developed a policy of meet-ing with parents after an evaluation (an exit interview) to give them my impressions and let them know some or all of the contents of the evaluation. I met with the mother first; the father was unable to meet with me until 9:30 P.M.

When he arrived, the building was virtually empty. He sat in front of me and wanted me to "cut to the chase," asking, "What are you recommending?"

A little hesitantly, but believing honesty was the best policy, I told him that I was recommending that visitation be suspended and that I did in fact believe that he had sexually abused his daughter.

There was a still quiet in the room and suddenly he pulled a gun. I sat there in disbelief and horror.

I had just been to a workshop on working with violent people, and the person who ran the workshop said that when someone pulls a gun you slowly and clearly ask that person to put the gun in your hand. All I could think of was what I had heard from the workshop presenter, and his admonition to avoid using abstract phrases like, "Give it to me."

I don't know how I was able to speak since my mouth was dry, but I looked at him, outstretched my hand and said, "I'd like you to place the gun in my hand"—at least I think that's what I said. His response was "Shit, no. We're just gonna sit here and talk about this some more."

From that point on I dissociated pretty heavily and seemed suspended in time, feeling my body fill with adrenaline, my palms sweat, and my face get cold. I tried to listen to what he said, but to this day can't repeat much of it. The gist was that I had made a mistake, that it was alright to make mistakes since the best of people do that, and that he wanted me to rectify my mistake by rethinking my recommendations.

At one point I did something really inappropriate. I stood up and went to the door, stating that it was late, and he could stay (*stay* in my office no less), but I had to go. (Apparently, when someone is pointing a gun at you it is not wise to stand. I didn't know that at this point.) He pinned me to the door and instructed me to take my seat again, since he wasn't finished with me.

I cannot describe the feeling (or lack of feeling) that one gets staring at that little hole pointing at you. From time to time I looked at him directly, avoiding the gun. Other times I wanted to look at the gun directly, as if to keep it from going off.

I could hear myself speaking, but I don't know how the thoughts were formed, or how I started this line of discussion, but I asked him to think about Lily, whom I knew he loved so much. I reiterated that I believed he loved his wife and child very much. I then asked him to visualize Lily growing up: birthdays, going to kindergarten, going to elementary school, her first ballet recital, roller-skating and riding bikes, playing softball, holding conversations, graduating first from grade school, then high school, then maybe college. The more I talked, the more he seemed mesmerized by what I was saying and the calm, rhythmic way I was speaking. He added events he looked forward to, and before I knew it, we were talking about his being a grandfather.

I looked at him boldly (I think it was boldly) and said, "If you shoot me, you'll miss out on all that." The gun lowered. "I ain't shooting anybody," he said, "but goddamn it, I don't want to lose them."

"Maybe that's something you can talk to your therapist about. You're not divorced yet. Anything is possible." I lied. His wife was adamant that she was divorcing him A.S.A.P.

I told him it was very late and I had to leave. I got up, opened the door, and told him he should go home also, and maybe he could call his therapist and make an appointment for the next day. He walked out the door and I sat and stared for about fifteen minutes. Leaving the building was one of the hardest things I have ever done.

This lesson was a tough one, but what I learned was to take what I do more seriously, to acknowledge the risk factors in some of what I do, and maybe even minimize the risk by screening more carefully the clients I see. I definitely changed my policy of "sharing" my recommendations with parents during court-mandated evaluations. I now submit my findings directly to the court and the court can share my findings.

I also meet with people during regular working hours, and I don't work in empty buildings at night.

I Want You to Be My Mom

This is a brief example of the potential dangers of overlooking the inherent danger that children will view clinicians as preferable to their parents.

In working with abusive families, there is always the potential that children will notice a marked difference between their parents' functioning (physical violence, inappropriate enmeshment and intrusion, or parental withdrawal of affection or nurturing) and the therapist's behavior. This difference is inevitable, given that we clinicians are trained to be sensitive, quiet, and concerned with the child's every thought and feeling, and we are not caretakers who provide a more broad range of interactions with children, including but not limited to conflictual, tense, or difficult ones.

In therapy, I focus on children's needs, I pay attention exclusively to them, I give them ample choice, I respect them, I treat them in a careful and considerate manner. Consequently, children can view therapy as safe and clinicians as helpers in the true sense of the word: individuals who have their best interests at heart. This clinical behavior is congruent with providing children with a reparative, corrective experience—something that balances the negative or hurtful experiences that precipitate referrals to treatment.

Sabrina was a five-year-old Caucasian child who had been physically abused and neglected. Her mother, Cora, was a woman in her thirties, who had a very low IQ that greatly compromised her ability to function in a job. Cora had been a welfare recipient most of her adult life, and found it very difficult to keep herself out of harm's way. When she had Sabrina, she was able to provide for her basic needs, and with the help of a public health nurse who visited twice a week and a protective services worker who oversaw the case and obtained extensive child care, Cora had been able to maintain her child's safety until Sabrina began to walk. At that point, Cora felt overwhelmed with the child's autonomy and was unable to respond to the child's growing need for constant supervision, stimulation, and attention.

Cora was frightened to go out alone, but at Sabrina's insistence, they went to the park together. During this outing, Cora "lost" Sabrina, and in a state of severe agitation, ran to the nearest police station. The police were quite concerned with the mother's volatility, and after locating the child a few blocks from the park, they referred the case to child protective services. At this point, child protective services removed the child to a foster home.

Cora became severely depressed, slept most of the day, cried incessantly, and would not eat or leave the house. She begged child protective services to return her child to her and promised she would get more help, attend parenting and counseling sessions, and take Sabrina to her day care facility. Child protective services was persuaded that Cora would provide sufficient safety and supervision, and after four months in foster care, Sabrina was returned home.

Cora's efforts were remarkable at first. However, she was frightened that her daughter would be removed from her again, and she despaired quickly when the child was crying or made strong demands.

Eventually, Cora decided that the only way she could keep Sabrina safe was to keep her under lock and key, and she began locking her in her room as soon as they got back from day care, in spite of loud protestations from Sabrina.

Cora had a limited attention span and was forgetful, and sometimes she would forget to let her daughter out for dinner. The child would sometimes sleep in her school clothes and be taken to school the next day in the same clothes. In addition, Cora had discovered that spanking Sabrina when she cried too long kept her quiet and compliant (she was afraid the neighbors would complain about her daughter's crying).

Unfortunately, a pattern of neglect and physical abuse unfolded slowly, and when Sabrina appeared hungry and told her teachers that she was not eating dinner regularly, the child was once again referred to protective services. Her bruises were not easily spotted because Cora instinctively knew to spank her child in nonvisible places such as the buttocks and back.

The mother had been seen at county mental health services for approximately ten years, and child protective services mandated that she reinitiate therapy, in spite of the fact that her previous therapist had retired and Cora was frightened about starting with someone new. Sabrina was once again removed to foster care, and referred to me for play therapy.

My countertransference responses to this child were as powerful as I have ever felt. She was a waiflike creature whose eyes told the whole story. She was a beautiful, open, trusting child who had lived with a parent who was incapacitated, erratic, and oftentimes brutal.

I worked with her for approximately nine months in play therapy. During that time she developed a strong attachment to me, since I was the first person who was consistent and reliable. (This child had had the bad fortune of entering a foster care environment in which she was physically abused by her foster mother; as a result, she did not view foster placements as necessarily stable or safe.)

She had remarkable abilities to use symbolic play and spent

most of her time with the dollhouse and the cooking utensils, both recreating a safe home environment in which the child took care of her sick mother (using doctor's medical bag, medicines, and so on), and constantly prepared food for her mother to eat. In doing so, I think this child was both expressing her real concern about her mother's inability to care for herself and her fear of not being cared for, nurtured, or fed herself.

Sabrina asked for her mother constantly during the first few months in therapy. Visitations were prohibited until recommendations were available from Cora's therapist as well as myself. Cora's psychologist and I agreed that it would be beneficial to both mother and child for visits to be instituted, and a plan of supervised visitation was ordered. Unfortunately, Cora was unable to get herself to scheduled supervised visits, and her inconsistent behavior troubled and scared the child.

I decided that part of the problem was that Cora lacked transportation, found it difficult to get around in buses, and was not always able to follow through on her intentions to see Sabrina. For those reasons, I felt that it was appropriate for me to pick up Cora and bring her to my office to see Sabrina, and to take her home afterwards. Although this was problematic to me, I felt that Cora would otherwise be unable to visit her child.

Their visits were touching. They played together as if they were playmates, and Sabrina always combed her mother's hair and examined her hands and arms for scratches. "You don't have boo-boos" she would say gladly to her mother on some visits, and yet other times when she noticed scratches she would say "Oh-oh, Oh-oh, boo-boos again," appearing to chastise her mother for scratching herself. The role-reversal was evident, as Cora was always given play foods to eat or allowed to play with toys first or complimented on her coloring. Cora obviously loved her child, but was really unable to provide for her adequately.

Transporting the mother back and forth gave me a chance to get to know her a little better. Slowly I developed a significant rapport with her, and she began to open up with me and talk to me about some of her problems, questions, and feelings. She did not like that Cora was far away, but conceded, "They feed her better at the other house." She could see that Cora looked pretty in her clean and ironed clothes and with ribbons in her hair. "She looks girly and nice," she would say. "She knows her ABCs."

I talked to Cora's therapist, who seemed frustrated at Cora's inability to make her regular appointments. I mentioned to her that Cora was able to get herself ready and be outside when someone came and transported her to her appointments. That obviously was not an option for Cora's therapist, and it was at this moment that I realized I had gotten overinvolved because I began thinking of transporting Cora to and from her therapy appointments.

Clearly, I had profound boundary problems with this case, compelled by an overwhelming desire to help Cora get the help she needed to become a better parent to my child client. Although I learned great lessons about having more exact boundaries with other clients, the more urgent clinical mistake came from overlooking the fact that Sabrina was becoming more and more attached to and dependent on me, which became painfully obvious the day she looked up at me and said, "I want you to be my mommy." Although many abused children view the therapist transferentially as "good mother," I had made inconsistent and nonassertive efforts at clarifying my role and encouraging the child to recognize and accept her mother's strengths as well as my shortcomings.

Furthermore, I found both mother and child compelling, and I wanted them to be able to live together safely. Somewhere inside of me I thought if I helped the mother "enough," she would be able to function adequately and meet the child's needs. However, what I ended up doing was overfunctioning, and as a result two things occurred: Cora underfunctioned even more than usual, and Sabrina viewed my efforts as confusing. I am sure Sabrina's statement about her desire that I "be" her mother came from confusion about my role—confusion due in part to the fact that I had become overinvolved with the family.

As a result of this experience, I am very cautious about clarifying my therapeutic role with children, and about making sure that no matter what their parents' deficits may be, the children also have a regard for their parents' strengths and efforts made on the children's behalf. In addition, I now recognize that overfunctioning for others often decreases their motivation to act on their own behalf, and in the long term is not a helpful approach. To do so creates a false illusion that the parent is helpless and cannot function independently.

A more helpful approach is to facilitate parental functioning by role modeling once or twice and then encouraging them to practice the desired behaviors, reviewing obstacles to completing the task or difficulties encountered. For example, rather than my transporting the mother to and from her and her daughter's appointments, it would have been more helpful to take the bus with her until she felt she could take public transportation safely by herself.

This case also taught me another important lesson: there are some people who cannot be helped to become safe, adequate, or consistent parents due to their incapacities. This child was placed in a long-term foster placement and had a diminishing number of visits with her mother as she grew older. Cora recognized that her daughter was happy and would often say, "We have two daughters," referring to the fact that Sabrina had two mothers. Sabrina's IQ was in normal range, and as she developed she seemed to recognize that her mother had special needs. I saw Sabrina periodically, either when the foster mother would call with a specific problem or when Sabrina had something she wanted to discuss with me.

The last time I saw Sabrina I bumped into her on the street. She was a freshman in high school. She told me that her mother was doing as well as could be expected, that she took her shopping from time to time, and that Cora came over to eat dinner "at her home" (the foster home) every other Sunday, although sometimes she forgot and showed up on a different day. Sabrina also reported that her mother was attending a program at the Regional Center, and did arts and crafts, and had met a group of friends she liked. Sabrina was a lovely, confident youngster, who acknowledged her mother's limitations, provided her with emotional support, and allowed professionals to help her in ways that her mother could not. She had transferred her loyalties to her consistent and loving foster parents, making room in her heart for an extended family system that included her biological mother and her substitute mother and father.

Colleagues have asked me some interesting questions, apparently intrigued by my exclusive commitment to working with child abuse. In particular, people have often asked me, "What got you involved in working with child abuse?"

I discovered the answer to that question last year.

I attended a conference and listened to a moving presentation by a Native American woman who chronicled the history of the Native American Indian and the horrendous actions perpetrated by Caucasians, intent on obliterating a culture they considered savage. This woman recounted how Native children were stripped from their families and sent to camps in which they were given Anglo names, not allowed to speak their native tongue, and forced to discard all visible symbols of their culture. It is no wonder, she mused, that many Native Americans lack a sense of identity and find themselves alienated from their ancestry.

As I listened to her speak, I was transported to my place of birth, Guayaquil, Ecuador, and I vividly recalled my own contact with its Indian population, and one small Indian girl who was relinquished by her family so that she might live with me as my companion and servant.

Her name was Chabita, and she and I were both seven years old. By accident, I had been born into a family of privilege; she was born poor and of "lower class." Her family valued her so much that they brought her to my grandmother so she could be raised in a home that could provide her with shelter, food, clothing, and educational opportunities.

Chabita cried desperately throughout the long nights. She slept on a blanket on the floor next to my bed. I tried to comfort her but she was inconsolable—she longed for her parents and siblings. We became closer and closer; as a matter of fact, I regarded her as the sister I had always wished for. Neither Chabita or myself understood at that point that we were perilously close to breaking cultural rules deeply imbedded in both our families.

Finally, my grandmother grew impatient with my desire to be with Chabita almost exclusively. She was my first great friend, and I clearly preferred her company to that of others.

Early one morning Chabita had fallen so deeply asleep in my arms that she was unable to get out of my warm bed before my grandmother came into the room. When my grandmother found Chabita in my bed she beat her and yelled at her for what seemed like an unbearable length of time. This was unfortunately one of many beatings I witnessed as my grandmother asserted cultural rules, against my feeble objections. Eventually, I realized that the only way to protect Chabita was to distance myself from her. And so our relationship was shaped into one that adhered to social dictates, with few stolen moments of joyous reunions.

I now know that Chabita is the reason I feel strongly about the protection and nurturing of children. I recognize that this desire to help those born into less fortunate or less nurturing situations stems directly from this early, formative experience. I only wish I had been able to find Chabita as an adult, to share with her how much she meant to me and how often I think of her these many years later and these many miles apart.

I believe that as interesting as the reason I and others choose to do this work is the reason we *continue* to do it, in spite of all the ups and downs, the stress, the challenge, and the deep and painful disappointments we experience when change is not sufficient to restore family functioning. I continue to do this work (after twenty-one years) because I have developed a level of confidence, comfort, and experience that allows me to make a contribution to some individuals, some of the time.

When I think about the state of the world, the injustices that persist, the pain, fear, and stress that surround modern living, and the plight of the disempowered or those oppressed by racism or struggling for equality, I despair. When I think about all the current social ills, I feel anxiety which can (and periodically does) debilitate me.

But I am quickly refocused when I work with one individual, one family, providing them with the benefit of my education and experience, helping them to help themselves and turn their lives around, so they can interact with each other free of violence and exploitation. Watching people change, thrive, and reach deep inside themselves to find resources they never knew were there is the reward that motivates me. So I continue to do the best I can, and every now and then I get a card from a child who has become an adolescent, and I listen to what the youngster is able to feel and express and I know I can and do make a difference, and that's why I continue to do this work.

My wish for you is that you persevere, empower yourself through education and experience, access your creativity, surround yourself with nurturing friends and family, trust the wisdom of your heart, soul, and mind, and cherish your rewards.

Appendix: Checklist for Reunification of Incestuous Families

Monica Roizner-Hayes

The purpose of this checklist is to assist professionals in making decisions about family reunification in cases of incestuous abuse by a parent. It should be completed by all treating professionals involved with the family members.

Rate the listed factors according to the following scale:

–3 = Very much against reunification

–2 = Against reunification

–1 = Slightly against reunification

 0 = Unclear/no information

 1 = Slightly in favor of reunification

 2 = In favor of reunification

 3 = Very much in favor of reunification

Uses

This checklist may be used for the following purposes:

1. Identification of risks/contraindications to reunification

2. Identification of child and parental strengths

3. Identification of areas of agreement and disagreement among professionals

4. Coordination of interventions among professionals

5. Determination of treatment goals at different stages of treatment

When several professionals' ratings are compared, they should be checked under P1, P2, or P3 to facilitate the comparison of ratings. Use by a single professional requires the availability of comprehensive information about all family members. This checklist can be used repeatedly at intervals to document progress and problems over time.

Family members' names and ages: *Professionals' names and roles:*

_____   P1 _____

_____   P2 _____

_____   P3 _____

Date of administration: _____   Proposed reevaluation date: _____

Child Factors

−3 = Very much against reunification; −2 = Against reunification; −1 = Slightly against reunification; 0 = Unclear/no information; 1 = Slightly in favor of reunification; 2 = In favor of reunification; 3 = Very much in favor of reunification

	P1	P2	P3	Description
1. Child's willingness and ability to report inappropriate behavior by offender				

	P1	P2	P3	Description

2. Child's available supports within the family

3. Child's current emotional functioning

4. Child's perception of nonoffending parent's ability to protect him or her in the future

5. Child's perception of the non-offending parent's views of the abuse

6. Child's comfort and safety in the presence of offender

7. Child's perception of offender's views of the abuse

8. Child's progress toward therapy goals

9. Child's available supports outside the family to whom she or he can report unacceptable parental behavior

10. Child's perception of nonoffending parent's ability to provide for his or her needs

11. Child's behavior after visits with the offender

12. Child's behavior toward the offender

13. Child's perception of offender's ability to provide for his or her needs

	P1	P2	P3	Description

14. Child's behavior after visits with the nonoffending parent

15. Child's behavior toward the non-offending parent

16. The specific issues that have been addressed in the child's therapy

17. Child's behavior prior to visits with offender

18. The child's therapist's views about the appropriateness of family reunification

19. Developmental considerations about the child

20. Child's behavior prior to visits with the nonoffending parent

21. Child's reaction to being away from his or her family

22. Child's cognitive functioning

23. Child's wishes about reunification

24. Child's attachment to offender

25. Child's emotional functioning at the time the abuse was disclosed

26. Type of therapy received by child

27. Length of time the child has been in therapy

28. Length of time the child has been in foster care

Offender Factors

−3 = Very much against reunification; −2 = Against reunification; −1 = Slightly against reunification; 0 = Unclear/no information; 1 = Slightly in favor of reunification; 2 = In favor of reunification; 3 = Very much in favor of reunification

	P1	P2	P3	Description

1. Offender's denial or acknowledgment of the facts of the abuse

2. Offender's denial or understanding of the effects of the abuse on the child

3. Offender's ability to put the child's interests and needs above his or her own

4. Offender's willingness to continue treatment after reunification

5. Offender's adherence to treatment recommendations

6. Offender's empathy for the child

7. Offender's progress toward behavioral goals

8. Appropriateness of offender's behavior toward the child during scheduled visits

9. Degree of remorse—or lack of it—for the abuse demonstrated by the offender

10. Offender's compliance with rules during visitation

	P1	P2	P3	Description

11. Offender's participation in recommended services

12. Offender's emotional functioning

13. Specific issues that had been addressed by offender in treatment

14. Offender's willingness to offer apologies and amends to the abused child

15. Offender's history of use of drugs or alcohol, including current status

16. Offender's history of domestic violence

17. Offender's acknowledgment and involvement in treatment for other problems

18. Offender's progress toward psychodynamic goals

19. Nature of offender's interpersonal relationships and supports

20. Offender's willingness to plead guilty in court for the abuse

21. Offender's therapist's views about his or her readiness to reunify

22. Offender's attendance to scheduled visits with the child

23. Offender's perception of current relationship with spouse

	P1	P2	P3	Description

24. Offender's parenting skills

25. Offender's cognitive functioning

26. Length of time offender has been in treatment

27. Type of therapy in which offender has participated

28. Offender's work history, including current work status

Nonoffending Parent Factors

–3 = Very much against reunification; –2 = Against reunification; –1 = Slightly against reunification; 0 = Unclear/no information; 1 = Slightly in favor of reunification; 2 = In favor of reunification; 3 = Very much in favor of reunification

	P1	P2	P3	Description

1. Nonoffending parent's ability to protect the child

2. Nonoffending parent's ability to confront the offender and report inappropriate behavior

3. Nonoffending parent's denial or acknowledgment of the facts of the abuse

4. Nonoffending parent's denial or acknowledgment of the effects of the abuse on the child

5. Nonoffending parent's adherence to treatment recommendations

P1   P2   P3   *Description*

6. Nonoffending parent's compliance and enforcement of recommended rules

7. Nonoffending parent's ability to put the child's interests and needs above his or her own

8. Nonoffending parent's empathy for the child

9. Nonoffending parent's ability to protect himself or herself

10. Appropriateness of nonoffending parent's behavior toward the child

11. Nonoffending parent's participation in recommended services

12. Nonoffending parent's history of drugs and alcohol, including current status

13. Nonoffending parent's emotional functioning

14. Nonoffending parent's progress toward behavioral goals

15. Nonoffending parent's having been a victim of domestic violence by the offender

16. Nonoffending parent's attendance to scheduled visits and appointments

	P1	P2	P3	Description

17. Nonoffending parent's perception of the relationship with his or her spouse

18. Nonoffending parent's parenting skills

19. Nonoffending parent's participation in recommended services

20. Nature of nonoffending parent's interpersonal relationships and supports

21. Nonoffending parent's actions (protective or not) when she or he learned about the abuse

22. Nonoffending parent's progress toward psychodynamic goals

23. Nonoffending parent's therapist's views about the family's reunification

24. Specific issues that have been addressed by nonoffending parent in treatment

25. Nonoffending parent's cognitive functioning

26. Type of therapy in which the nonoffending parent has participated

27. Length of time the nonoffending parent has been in treatment

	P1	P2	P3	*Description*

28. Nonoffending parent's work history, including current work status

Assessment Instruments

Sources of Assessment Instruments

Adolescent Abuse Inventory (taps parental commitment to abusive versus nonabusive responses to adolescent behavior): J. M. Sebes, *Determining Risk for Abuse in Families with Adolescents. The Development of a Criterion Measure.* Unpublished doctoral dissertation. University Park: Pennsylvania State University, 1983.

A-FILE (assesses stressful life changes): D. H. Olson, *FACES.* St. Paul: Family Social Services, University of Minnesota, 1985.

Child Abuse Potential Inventory: J. S. Milner, *The Child Abuse Potential Inventory Manual.* Webster, N. C.: Psytec Corp., 1980, 1986.

Conflict Tactics Scale (measures physical abuse): M. A. Straus, *Measuring Psychological Abuse of Children with the Conflict Tactics Scale.* Durham: University of New Hampshire, Family Research Laboratory, 1989.

FACES (assesses family adaptability and cohesion): D. H. Olson, *FACES.* St. Paul: Family Social Services, University of Minnesota, 1985.

Parent-Child Interaction Form: D. A. Wolfe et al. *The Child Management Program for Abusive Parents.* Winter Park, Fla.: Anna, 1981.

Parenting Stress Index: R. Abidin, *The Parenting Stress Index,* Charlottesville, Virg.: Pediatric Psychology Press, 1983.

Parent Interview and Assessment Guide: D. A. Wolfe, *Preventing Physical and Emotional Abuse of Children* (table 4.1, p. 67). New York: Guilford Press, 1991.

Purdue Sex History Form: T. S. Trepper and M. J. Barrett, *Systemic Treatment of Incest: A Therapeutic Handbook* (appendix). New York: Bruner/Mazel, 1989.

Vulnerability to Incest Model (structures assessment of vulnerability to incest): T. S. Trepper and M. J. Barrett, *Systemic Treatment of Incest: A Therapeutic Handbook* (ch. 2). New York: Bruner/Mazel, 1989.

Other Sources of Assessment Discussion

D. Jehu, *Beyond Sexual Abuse* (chs. 6, 12, 22). New York: John Wiley & Sons, 1988.

J. W. Maddock et al., "An Evaluation Protocol for Incest Family Functioning," in M. Q. Patton (ed.), *Family Sexual Abuse: Frontline Research and Evaluation*. Newbury Park, Calif.: Sage Publications, 1991.

C. M. Newberger, "Psychology and Child Abuse," in E. H. Newberger (ed.), *Child Abuse*. Boston: Little, Brown, 1982.

T. S. Trepper and M. J. Barrett, *Systemic Treatment of Incest: A Therapeutic Handbook* (ch. 6). New York: Bruner/Mazel, 1989.

T. S. Trepper and M. J. Barrett (eds.). *Treating Incest: A Multiple Systems Perspective*. New York: Haworth Press, 1986.

References

Abel, G., and others. "Self-Reported Sex Crimes on Non-incarcerated Paraphilias." *Journal of Interpersonal Violence,* 1987, *1,* 3–25.

Azar, S. T., and Wolfe, D. A. "Child Abuse and Neglect." In E. J. Mash and R. A. Barkley (eds.), *Treatment of Childhood Disorders.* New York: Guilford Press, 1989.

Bedrosian, R. C., and Bozicas, G. D. *Treating Family of Origin Problems: A Cognitive Approach.* New York: Guilford Press, 1994.

Belsky, J. "Child Maltreatment: An Ecological Integration." *American Psychologist,* 1980, *35,* 320–335.

Berg, I. K. *Family-Based Services: A Solution-Focused Approach.* New York: Norton, 1994.

Berliner, L. "Removing the Offenders in Cases of Family Sexual Assault." *ATSA News,* 1986, *5*(3).

Bonner, B. L., Kaufman, K. L., Harbeck, C., and Brassard, M. R. "Child Maltreatment." In C. E. Walker and M. C. Roberts (eds.), *Handbook of Clinical Child Psychology.* New York: Wiley, 1992.

Bronfenbrenner, J. "Toward an Experimental Ecology of Human Development." *American Psychologist,* 1977, *32,* 513–531.

Chaffin, M. "Assessment and Treatment of Child Sexual Abusers." *Journal of Interpersonal Violence,* 1994, *9*(2), 224–237.

Cicchetti, D., and Carlson, V. *Child Maltreatment: Theory and Research on the Causes and Consequences of Child Abuse and Neglect*. New York: Cambridge University Press, 1989.

Coleman, S. B. (ed.). *Failures in Family Therapy*. New York: Guilford Press, 1985.

Cormier, B. N., Kennedy, M., and Sancowicz, J. "Psychodynamics of Father-Daughter Incest." In C. D. Bryant and J. G. Wells (eds.), *Deviance and the Family*. Philadelphia: Davis, 1973.

Drotar, D. "Prevention of Neglect and Nonorganic Failure to Thrive." In D. J. Willis, E. W. Holden, and M. Rosenberg (eds.), *Prevention of Child Maltreatment: Developmental and Ecological Perspectives*. New York: John Wiley, 1992.

Elmer, E. "Identification of Abused Children." *Children*, 1963, *10*, 180–184.

Finkelhor, D. *Child Sexual Abuse*. New York: Free Press, 1984.

Finkelhor, D. *A Sourcebook in Child Sexual Abuse*. Beverly Hills, Calif.: Sage Publications, 1986.

Finkelhor, D. "The Sexual Abuse of Children: Current Research Reviewed." *Psychiatric Annals*, 1987, *17*(4), 233–241.

Fish, V., and Faynik, C. "Treatment of Incest Families with the Father Temporarily Removed: A Structural Approach." *Journal of Strategic and Systemic Therapies*, 1989, 8(4), 53–63D.

Friedrich, W. N. *Psychotherapy of Sexually Abused Children and Their Families*. New York: Norton, 1990.

Fritz, M. E. "Full Circle Forward." *Child Abuse and Neglect*, 1989, *13*, 313–318.

Garbarino, J. "Healing the Social Wounds of Isolation." In E. H. Newberger (ed.), *Child Abuse*. Boston: Little, Brown and Co., 1982.

Garbarino, J. "The Human Ecology of Child Maltreatment: A Conceptual Model for Research." *Journal of Marriage and the Family*, 1977, *39*, 721–727.

Gelles, R. J. "Child Abuse and Family Violence: Implications for Medical Professionals." In E. H. Newberger (ed.), *Child Abuse*. Boston: Little, Brown and Co., 1982.

Gelles, R. J. "Child Protection Needs to Replace Family Reunification as Goal of Child Welfare Agencies." *The Brown University Family Therapy Journal*, 1992, 4(6), 1–2.

Gelles, R. "The Doctrine of Family Reunification: Child Protection or Risk?" *The APSAC Advisor,* 1993, 6(2), 9–11.

Gelles, R. Presentation at American Professional Society on Abuse of Children Annual Colloqium, Cambridge, Mass., 1994.

Giarretto, H. *Integrated Treatment of Child Sexual Abuse: A Treatment and Training Manual.* Palo Alto, Calif.: Human Sciences and Behavior Books, 1982.

Herman, J. L. *Father-Daughter Incest.* Cambridge, Mass.: Harvard University Press, 1981.

Herman, J. L. *Trauma and Recovery.* New York: Basic Books, 1992.

Holden, E. W., Willis, D. J., and Corcoran, M. "Preventing Child Maltreatment During the Prenatal/Perinatal Period." In D. J. Willis, E. W. Holden, and M. Rosenberg (eds.), *Prevention of Child Maltreatment: Developmental and Ecological Perspectives.* New York: John Wiley, 1992.

Karen, R. *Becoming Attached: Unfolding the Mystery of the Infant-Mother Bond and Its Impact on Later Life.* New York: Warner Books, 1994.

Maisch, H. *Incest.* New York: Stein and Day, 1972.

Maluccio, A. N., Waarsh, R., and Pine, B. A. "Family Reunification: An Overview." In A. B. Pine, R. Krieger, and A. N. Maluccio (eds.), *Together Again: Family Reunification in Foster Care.* Washington, D.C.: Child Welfare League of America, 1993.

Meinig, M. B., and Bonner, B. L. "Returning the Treated Sex Offender to the Family." *Violence Update,* 1990, *1*(2), 3–11.

Merrill, E. J. "Physical Abuse of Children: An Agency Study." In V. DeFrances (ed.), *Protecting the Battered Child.* Denver, Co.: American Humane Association, 1962.

National Research Council. *Understanding Child Abuse and Neglect.* Washington, D.C.: National Academy Press, 1993.

O'Connell, M. A. "Reuniting Incest Offenders with Their Families." *Journal of Interpersonal Violence,* 1986, *1*(3), 374–386.

Orenchuk-Tomiuk, N., Matthey, G., and Pigler Christensen, C. "The Resolution Model: A Comprehensive Treatment Framework in Sexual Abuse." *Child Welfare,* 1990, *2019*(5), 417–431.

Orten, J. D., and Rich, L. L. "A Model for Assessment of Incestuous Families." *Social Casework: The Journal of Contemporary Social Work,* Dec. 1988, 611–619.

Paul, H. *Family Circle*. 16468 Dorado, Encino, Calif., 91436–4118. (818) 501–0055, 1981.

Pence, D. M. "Family Preservation and Reunification in Intrafamilial Sexual Abuse Cases: A Law Enforcement Perspective." *Journal of Child Sexual Abuse*, 1993, 2(2), 103–108.

Powell, G. F., Low, J. L., and Spears, M. A. "Behavior as a Diagnostic Aid in Failure to Thrive." *Journal of Developmental and Behavioral Pediatrics*, 1987, 4, 26–33.

Radbill, S. X. "A History of Child Abuse and Infanticide." In R. E. Helfer and C. H. Kempe, *The Battered Child*, 2nd. ed., Chicago, Ill.: University of Chicago Press, 1974.

Raphling, D. L., Carpenter, B. L., and Davis, A. "Incest: A Genealogical Study." *Archives of General Psychiatry*, 1967, 16, 505–511.

Roizner-Hayes, M. "Therapists' Attitudes Towards the Reunification of Incestuous Families After Treatment." Unpublished doctoral dissertation, Boston University, 1994.

Server, J. C., and Janzen, C. "Contraindications to Reconstitution of Sexually Abusive Families." *Child Welfare*, 1982, 61, 270–288.

Smith, T. "When Is It Safe to Allow an Offender to Return to the Home?" *National Resource Center on Child Sexual Abuse of the National Center on Child Abuse and Neglect*, 1994, 3(2), 3.

Steele, B. F., and Pollock, C. B. "A Psychiatric Study of Parents Who Abuse Infants and Small Children." In R. E. Helfer and C. H. Kempe (eds.), *The Battered Child*. Chicago: University of Chicago Press, 1968.

Stickrod Gray, A., and Pithers, W. D. "Relapse Prevention with Sexually Aggressive Adolescents and Children: Expanding Treatment and Supervision." In H. E. Barbaree, W. M. Marshall, and S. M. Hudson. *Juvenile Sex Offender*. New York: Guilford Press, 1993.

Straus, M. A., and Gelles, R. J. "Societal Change in Family Violence from 1975 to 1985 as Revealed by Two National Surveys." *Journal of Marriage and the Family*, 1986, 48, 465–479.

Tinbergen, N. *The Study of Instinct*. London: Oxford University Press, 1951.

Trepper, T., and Barrett, M. J. *Systemic Treatment of Incest: A Therapeutic Handbook*. New York: Brunner/Mazel, 1989.

Vander Mey, B. J., and Neff, R. L. *Incest as Child Abuse: Research and Applications*. New York: Praeger, 1986.

Walker, L. E. A. *The Battered Woman*. New York: Harper & Row, 1979.

Wolfe, D. A. *Child Abuse: Implications for Child Development and Psychopathology*. Beverly Hills, Calif.: Sage, 1987.

Wolfe, D. A. *Preventing Physical and Emotional Abuse of Children*. New York: Guilford Press, 1991.

Wolfner, G., and Gelles, R. J. "A Profile of Violence Against Children: A National Study." *Child Abuse and Neglect*, 1993, *17*(2) 197–212.

About the Authors

ELIANA GIL is a licensed marriage, family, and child counselor, and a registered play therapy supervisor. She specializes in the treatment of abused children, their families, and adult survivors. She is director of the Center for Advanced Clinical Development, a program of the Multicultural Clinical Centers in Springfield, Virginia, where she provides educational and clinical services. Gil is on the boards of directors of both the American Professional Society on the Abuse of Children and the National Resource Center on Child Sexual Abuse. She is the author of numerous books, including *Play in Family Therapy, Sexualized Children: Assessment and Treatment of Sexualized Children and Children Who Molest, The Healing Power of Play: Working with Abused Children*. Gil is bilingual, bicultural, and originally from Guayaquil, Ecuador. She obtained her Ph.D. in marital and family therapy from the California Graduate School of Family Psychology in San Rafael, California, in 1982.

MONICA ROIZNER-HAYES coauthored Chapter Five, on family reunification. Roizner-Hayes obtained her Ed.D. in 1994 in counseling psychology at the Boston University School of Education. She has consulted and lectured extensively both nationally and internationally on sexual abuse, child abuse, trauma, interdisciplinary interventions, cross-cultural psychology, and Latino mental health. She is currently a coordinator on the Boston Sexual Abuse Team. Roizner-Hayes has also coordinated and served on several sexual abuse teams throughout Massachusetts, and has conducted research in the area of reunification of incestuous families. She is on the board of directors of the Massachusetts Chapter of the American Professional Society on the Abuse of Children.

Index